Luther on Leadership

Luther on Leadership

Leadership Insights from the Great Reformer

Edited by
DAVID D. COOK

Introduction by Brent Ashton Thomason

WIPF & STOCK · Eugene, Oregon

LUTHER ON LEADERSHIP

Copyright © 2017 Wipf and Stock Publishers. All rights reserved. Except for brief quotations in critical publications or reviews, no part of this book may be reproduced in any manner without prior written permission from the publisher. Write: Permissions, Wipf and Stock Publishers, 199 W. 8th Ave., Suite 3, Eugene, OR 97401.

Wipf & Stock
An Imprint of Wipf and Stock Publishers
199 W. 8th Ave., Suite 3
Eugene, OR 97401

www.wipfandstock.com

PAPERBACK ISBN: 978-1-5326-3526-7
HARDCOVER ISBN: 978-1-5326-3528-1
EBOOK ISBN: 978-1-5326-3527-4

Manufactured in the U.S.A.   12/04/17

Scripture quotations are from the ESV® Bible (The Holy Bible, English Standard Version®), copyright © 2001 by Crossway, a publishing ministry of Good News Publishers. Used by permission. All rights reserved

Contents

Contributors | vii
Introduction | ix
 Dr. Brent A. Thomason

Section 1: The Legacy of Martin Luther and the Reformation

1 Luther's Life and Theology | 3
 Dr. Brent A. Thomason

2 Faith, Scripture, and Vocation: The Spiritual Legacies of Martin Luther on Protestant Evangelicalism | 18
 Dr. Michael Whiting

3 Martin Luther's Influence on Politics, the Law, Education, and Economics | 33
 Dr. David D. Cook

4 Martin Luther's Impact on Church-State Relations in the West | 54
 Dr. Jack Goodyear

Section 2: Assessing Martin Luther's Leadership

5 Martin Luther's Leadership as a Change Agent | 71
 Dr. David D. Cook

6 Luther as an Adaptive Leader | 87
 Dr. Erik Gronberg

7 Luther as a Transformational Leader | 102
 Dr. Jay Harley

8 Luther's Pastoral Leadership | 121
 Mark A. Cook

9 Luther as a Servant Leader | 136
   Dr. Justin Gandy

Epilogue | 149
   Dr. David D. Cook

Bibliography | 151

Contributors

David D. Cook, assistant professor of leadership at Dallas Baptist University.

Mark Cook, assistant professor of biblical studies and leadership at Dallas Baptist University.

Justin Gandy, associate professor of management at Dallas Baptist University.

Jack Goodyear, dean of the Cook School of Leadership at Dallas Baptist University.

Erik Gronberg, bishop of the Northern Texas-Northern Louisiana Synod of the Evangelical Lutheran Church in America.

Jay Harley, vice president for student affairs at Dallas Baptist University.

Brent Thomason, assistant professor of biblical studies at Dallas Baptist University.

Michael Whiting, assistant professor of Christian history and leadership at Dallas Baptist University.

Introduction

Dr. Brent A. Thomason

The year 2017 commemorates the quincentennial celebration of Martin Luther's nailing the *95 Theses* to the door of the *Schlosskirche* in Wittenberg, Germany, on October 31, 1517. Germany has long anticipated the frenzy of 2017 precipitated inevitably by the Reformation zealots flooding the central German uplands, tracing the steps of the monk-rebel turned married-Reformer. In preparation for the tourist swell, many of the *Lutherdänkmale* have been revived and *Lutherhäuser* renovated.[1] Publishers too have capitalized on the stir-crazy Reformation scholars who strategically released new research on Luther or revised and updated seminal works this year.[2] So why yet another book on Luther in an already inundated market? We commend the stalwart Baintons[3] and Kittelsons[4] of Reformation research who have exhausted the life and career of Martin Luther. Similarly, the Althauses[5] and Lohses[6] among Luther scholars have treated Dr. Luther's theology thoroughly. But when it came time to tip the proverbial hat to those who have analyzed Luther through the relatively new lens of leadership theories, there were few standing on the world stage. Thus we have undertaken the task of uniquely evaluating the leadership qualities of Martin Luther through the integration of various contemporary leadership theories in the expanding field of leadership

---

1. Cf., e.g., *Lutherhaus* Wittenberg.
2. Kittelson and Wiersma, *Luther the Reformer*; Hendrix, *Martin Luther*; Pettegree, *Unheralded Monk*.
3. Bainton, *Here I Stand*.
4. Kittelson and Wiersma, *Luther the Reformer*.
5. Althaus, *Theology of Martin Luther*.
6. Lohse, *Martin Luther's Theology*.

studies to draw attention to this Reformer's style of trailblazing the German Reformation.

To this end, part 1 of the book examines the legacy of Martin Luther and the Reformation. The first chapter acquaints the reader with the life and theology of Luther.[7] Though its brevity is clearly a disservice to Luther's life, the chapter overviews the journey of Luther with sufficient time dedicated to certain episodes of his life which demonstrate Luther's leadership. Further, the tenets of Luther's convictions which shaped his style(s) of leadership in the Reformation are outlined in the "Five Pillars" of his theology. Building upon this, the next chapter explores the spiritual legacy of the Reformation.[8] Strides are made to show how Luther's theology left an impact on Protestantism and a spiritual heritage for the priesthood of the believer, empowering laypeople's personal relationship with God and securing their dignity in service to the world. Next, the book turns to assess Luther's influence on various facets of society[9] and his impact on church-state relations.[10] With reference to the former, Luther's deeply held religious beliefs spill over into politics, education, city governance, and economics. Even if at times these were the unintended consequences of his Reformation, nothing in society could hide from Luther's transformational quill. Regarding the latter, Luther's proto-"Two Kingdoms" doctrine profoundly affected the direction of the church-state separation development. Understanding both are to be submissive to God, Luther drew up strict restrictions to the reach of the ecclesiastical and political arms.

Next, the book shifts gears to part 2 where Luther's leadership is more closely evaluated utilizing the growing canon of leadership studies literature. First, Luther is analyzed as a change agent using John Kotter's Eight-Step Model of Change.[11] Luther is shown to be a catalyst for changing the very fabric of European society. His beliefs and actions served as an inflection point, changing the trajectory of German, and later Protestant, culture. Afterward, Luther's skills as an adaptive leader are scrutinized using the seminal work of Ronald Heifetz.[12] The winds of change precipitated by the Reformation forced

---

7. See Brent Thomason's chapter in this volume, "The Life and Theology of Martin Luther" (ch. 1).

8. See Michael Whiting's chapter in this volume, "Faith, Scripture, and Vocation: The Spiritual Legacies of Martin Luther on Protestant Evangelicalism" (ch. 2).

9. See David Cook's chapter in this volume, "Martin Luther's Influence on Politics, Education, the Law, and Economics" (ch. 3).

10. See Jack Goodyear's chapter in this volume, "Martin Luther's Impact on Church-State Relations in the West" (ch. 4).

11. See David Cook's chapter in this volume, "Martin Luther's Leadership as a Change Agent" (ch. 5).

12. See Erik Gronberg's chapter in this volume, "Luther as an Adaptive Leader" (ch. 6).

Luther, along with his German comrades, to find adaptive solutions to the structural gaps created in the blossoming Protestant movement. Truly, Luther will be shown to exhibit the traits of an adaptive leader. What follows is a review of Martin Luther's transformational leadership as explained through the works of James MacGregor Burns and Bernard Bass.[13] Luther's charismatic personality modeled poignantly the four elements of a transformational leader: individualized consideration, intellectual stimulation, inspirational motivation, and idealized influence. Next, attention is paid to Luther's pastoral leadership among his students, the poor, and the children of the Reformation.[14] Viewing himself more as a pastor than a Reformer, Luther's theology shaped his unwavering convictional views of the pastor's calling, purpose, and task in the parish. Luther's influence on his followers, the Protestant movement, and Western world still sends shockwaves five hundred years after the penning of the 95 *Theses*. Finally, Luther's servant leadership is highlighted.[15] By remaining in tune with his followership, and guided by the convictions of Holy Writ alone, Luther accurately assessed and met the needs of his disciples, becoming a quintessential biblical servant leader.

But before an investigation of Luther's leadership gets underway, a word ought to be said about the times into which Luther was born and through which Luther led. The late fifteenth and early sixteenth centuries have been described as "nasty, brutish, and short."[16] The Black Death had already ravaged Europe leaving in its wake one- to two-thirds of its population as corpses. Infant mortality rates reached 60 percent within the first six months of life. Annually, beggars in the Rhineland were rounded up and driven off the banks into the river.[17] If one were privileged to grow up in a stable home, he would have been reared with a firm hand, a wooden rod, and other forms of strict discipline. The barbaric times forged cast-iron wills and calloused skin. Luther would need it!

Compounding the harshness of the times was the spiritual condition of the land. On the one hand, superstition ran rampant. It was not uncommon to think that a curse rested upon the marriage union of a monk and nun, so that even Luther's own parents assumed the child born to Martin and Katharina von Bora would have two heads.[18] As a child, Martin's mother blamed the

---

13. See Jay Harley's chapter in this volume, "Luther as a Transformational Leader" (ch. 7).
14. See Mark Cook's chapter in this volume, "Luther's Pastoral Leadership" (ch. 8).
15. See Justin Gandy's chapter in this volume, "Luther as a Servant Leader" (ch. 10).
16. Kittelson and Wiersma, *Luther the Reformer*, 5.
17. Ibid., 4–5.
18. Thigpen, "Family Album," 15.

death of one of her sons on the "witch" who lived next door, betraying the unfounded beliefs of her day.[19] On the other hand, the established religion of the medieval Catholic Church was both spiritually deficient, due to its works-based salvation, and scandalized, due to the corruption of the clergy, whether from the abuse of indulgence selling or the sexual promiscuity of priests in Rome, for instance.[20] These were spiritually dark days. Luther, like many others, imbibed the religion around him till he was drunk with the cheap doctrines of the church.[21] It would take the Word of God to sober him from his papal intoxication.

These bleak times were not without hope though. A spirit of conquest, opportunity, and expression penetrated even the darkest corner and dirtiest mud-caked cheeks of children aimlessly wandering the streets. For out of this Renaissance era Columbus discovered the Americas, da Vinci painted the Last Supper and the Mona Lisa, Michelangelo commenced work on the Sistine Chapel, and Copernicus revolutionized the way the educated elite viewed the center of the universe. The map of humanity was expanding. Black and white sketches gave way to multicolored tapestries. And the world stage was set for Luther to make his debut.

Among many contributing factors to Luther's debut success as the German Reformation leader, three were Desiderius Erasmus's Greek New Testament, Johann Tetzel's abuse of selling indulgences, and Johannes Gutenberg's invention of the printing press. The Renaissance Humanism mantra *ad fontes* drove Erasmus to complete the *Novum Instrumentum omne* (1516) which in turn led Luther to discover for the first time the words of Jesus in Matthew 4:17, μετανοῖτε ("repent ye"), rather than the Latin's, *pœnitentiam agite* ("do penance"). Erasmus had understood the Greek's implication of the changing of the mind rather than an outward, and face-to-face, act of penance with a priest, and so he revised the Latin Vulgate at this point to read *resipiscite*. Erasmus's Greek edition of the New Testament, along with his alternative translational rendering of Jesus's words, and the early ruminations on "justification by faith" which were borne out of Luther's lectures on Romans (1515–16), set in motion the German Reformer's questioning the legitimacy of the selling of indulgences and other late medieval church doctrine. This questioning, though resting relatively dormant until the onset of Johann Tetzel, helped lay the foundation of the German monk's Reformation.

The seeds of doubt that had been planted in the mind of Luther as a result of Erasmus's new Greek and Latin translations germinated when Luther

19. Kittelson, "Accidental Revolutionary," 10.
20. Kittelson and Wiersma, *Luther the Reformer*, 25.
21. Kittelson, "Accidental Revolutionary," 12.

encountered Johann Tetzel employing the heretical motto, "Once the coin in the coffer rings, a soul from purgatory heavenward springs."[22] Luther was sickened by the abuse of indulgence selling. Pope Leo X's support of such gimmickry to finance the building of St. Peter's Basilica in Rome, which Luther deemed nothing short of racketeering, caused the buds of Luther's convictions to bloom and found their first expression in the 95 *Theses* that Luther nailed to the Castle Church door in Wittenberg. The unintended consequences of Tetzel's indulgence-racketeering business to raise funds for the construction of St. Peter's Basilica was the beginnings of the exodus of Europeans from the Catholic Church as they followed Luther et al. into the promised land of Protestantism. The Reformation had begun; *es gab kein Zurück!*[23]

It is said that Luther never intended for his 95 *Theses* to go viral.[24] The objections he penned in the 95 *Theses* were an attempt to dispute Tetzel and others in the environs of Wittenberg, not take on continental Europe. But Johannes Gutenberg's printing press would have the final say. And speak it did! If Luther were the match, the printing press was the powder keg. Luther's *Disputatio* were published without his permission and within two weeks had spread throughout Germany. Europe was spiritually famished and Luther's theses satisfied the soul. Within six months the 95 *Theses* had spanned the continent.[25] Gutenberg's ancient mass-media mechanism churned out copies of Luther's works faster than he could pen them.[26] Though at times lamenting this predicament,[27] Luther understood the value of the printing press and

22. Ibid., 14.

23. Transl.: "There was no turning back."

24. Brown, "Preaching from the Print Shop," 33. Six months later, on May 30, 1518, Luther explained to Pope Leo X, "It is a mystery to me how my theses . . . were spread to so many places. They were meant exclusively for our academic circle here" (Hillerbrand, *Protestant Reformation*, 54).

25. Ibid., 33.

26. That is astonishing considering that Luther translated the New Testament into German at a rate of 1,500 words per day (Jacobsen, "Did You Know?," 2). At the end of his career, Luther had penned over four hundred works, some 60,000 words contained in 55 volumes in English! (Robbert, "Recommended Resources," 51).

27. Brown, "Profit-Hungry Printers," 34: His letter to friend Georg Spalatin in August 1521 reveals Luther's exasperation that his crafted "Sermon on Confession" had been hastily hacked at the press by a profit-hungry publisher: "I cannot say how sorry and disgusted I am with the printing. I wish I had sent nothing in German, because they print it so poorly, carelessly, and confusedly, to say nothing of bad types and paper. John the printer is always the same old Johnny. Please do not let him print any of my German homilies, but return them for me to send elsewhere. . . . I shall forward no more until I learn that these sordid mercenaries care less for their profits than for the public. Such printers seem to think: 'It is enough for me to get the money; let the readers look out for the matter'" (*Luther's Works*, 48:291; subsequent citations of *Luther's Works* will be abbreviated *LW*

admitted it was "God's highest and extremist act of grace, whereby the business of the Gospel is driven forward."[28] The Gutenberg press fanned into flame Luther's fiery words setting Europe ablaze.

Leaders are not born in a vacuum nor formed in isolation. The circumstances surrounding Luther's life culminated in the forging of a leader who was as courageous as Joshua, rhetorical as Cicero, contemplative as Augustine, and rebellious as Spartacus. The situations of his life which gave rise to the convictions with which he led is the subject that we turn to next.

---

followed by the volume and page number).

28. Brown, "Preaching from the Print Shop," 33.

SECTION 1

The Legacy of Martin Luther and the Reformation

1

Luther's Life and Theology

Dr. Brent A. Thomason

Though some have undertaken the task of dissecting Luther's theology from his life experiences, and vice versa, this chapter's goal is to recount the life and experiences which bore out the convictions of a man who could do no other than to stand unwaveringly on certain theological precepts. The current presentation of Martin Luther is not intended to be exhaustive—superior volumes have been dedicated to that purpose. However, select episodes from Martin's life have been recounted here insofar as the author believes these life experiences shaped Luther's personal and theological convictions, which in turn are scrutinized in the following chapters as these convictions came to bear on Luther's leadership contributions.

THE REFORMER'S FOUNDATIONAL YEARS

Martin Luther was born the second son to Hans and Margaretta Luder on November 10, 1483, in Eisleben, Germany. He was baptized in the local church the next day and given the name "Martin" after the celebration of the Feast of St. Martin on November 11, 1483. Hans was a peasant and did not fare well in Eisleben. Uprooting the Luder family, Hans moved to Mansfield where he found work in the copper mines. Within seven years, the Luder family

Section 1: The Legacy of Martin Luther and the Reformation

prospered, relatively speaking, in that Hans owned his own copper mining business.[1]

Martin grew up in a very strict and disciplined home, though not very different from other young boys of his time. Disciplining young Luther flowed from the strict expectations by which Hans and Margaretta held themselves. Though contemporaries with Copernicus, Christopher Columbus, and Michelangelo, the explorations and advancements brought about by the Renaissance era were immaterial to the peasant-living of the Luder family. The discipline of the family ensured a practical approach to eking out a livelihood for the young Luther. With infant mortality rates soaring to 60 percent, and adulthood facing the treacherous life of revolts and feuds with landlords, not to mention the Plague, syphilis and "English Sweats" which ravaged the European continent, it was imperative that Martin find passage out of the hostility and frailty of peasant life. Thus, Hans decided to send Martin on an educational journey.

At the age of five, Martin attended Latin School in Mansfield. Over the course of eight years, he learned Latin, music, and a few catechisms. The school was brutish and Martin learned primarily from coercion rather than the joy of accruing knowledge. Caning was a common disciplinary method for young boys like Martin who had not learned their Latin grammar tables. At age thirteen, Martin was sent away to Magdeburg where he exercised his music skills through caroling in the streets among young boys—a common practice to acquire food and drink. The following year, in 1498, Martin was sent to school in Eisenach where his street caroling found the favor of a wealthy woman who provided him the amenities of a comfortable life. The three years spent at Eisenach were transformational for Luther. His Latin skills excelled, learning to give oration in Latin and read the ancients in the same.[2] His skill found the eye of the school's headmaster John Trebonius who recommended to Hans that Martin be sent away to the University of Erfurt at seventeen years old. Up to this point, Martin experienced a normal education and did not stand out among his peers insofar as boys attended school. What would have been unusual about his upbringing was that his modest home roots afforded him such an opportunity to attend university instead of taking over the family business.

---

1. By the time Luther was 25, the Luder family owned six mine shafts and two copper smelters.

2. A parchment piece was found on Luther's person at the time of his death. An excerpt read, "No one can understand Virgil in his Bucolics unless he has been a herdsman for five years. No one can understand Virgil in his Georgics unless he has been a farmer for five years. No one can fully understand Cicero in his letters unless he has spent twenty-five years in a great commonwealth" (Edwards, "After the Revolution," 13).

These foundational years instilled in Luther the strong sense of discipline and perfection in his work ethic. Luther's strict upbringing found expression in the way he agonized over each choice of word translated from the Bible's original languages to the vernacular German. Luther at times spent up to a month contemplating the most fitting translation of one word, taking pains even to visit a butcher shop to better translate the priestly sacrificial processes.[3] Though far superior in their grasp of the language, the team of Hebrew scholars Luther commissioned for the translation of the Old Testament had to pass every word through the scrutiny of Luther's litmus test.[4] His disciplined childhood even found an outlet of expression in the thoroughness of his confessions as a young monk. Luther daily cross-examined his heart with such vigor, recounting even the minutest sin to his Augustinian order, that Johann von Staupitz once remarked, "You want to be without sin, but you don't have any real sins anyway . . . the murder of one's parents, public vices, blasphemy, adultery, and the like. These are sins. . . . You must not inflate your halting, artificial sins out of proportion!"[5] Years of cultivating a disciplined life in his primary years bore the quality traits which shaped the rigorous leader Luther was bound to become.

THE REFORMER'S TRANSFORMATIONAL YEARS

At university, Luther proved to be a model student, standing head and shoulders above his peers.[6] Luther so excelled in the late medieval education of the trivium (grammar, rhetoric, and dialectic) that he earned the nickname "The Philosopher" among his peers. He devoured the curriculum at a neck-breaking speed, completing his bachelor of arts and master of arts in the shortest time possible—two years for the former and three years for the latter. At that time, Hans made the farsighted decision to provide for his family by sending Master Martin to law school. If Martin succeeded, the Luder family estate would be secure. Hans even purchased the very costly, central law text of the time for Martin—the *Corpus Juris Civilis*. But Luther's law career was not meant to be.

3. Zecher, "Bible Translation," 36.

4. Luther dubbed his team of translators the "Sanhedrin": Philipp Melanchthon, Justus Jonas, John Bugenhagen, and Caspar Cruciger. Luther was a trailblazer in this too in that his Bible translation committee formed the precedent for modern editorial committees of the Bible. For Luther, the word choice had to sound right, for "faith comes from hearing and hearing through the word of Christ." See Romans 10:7.

5. Kittelson, "Accidental Revolutionary," 12.

6. Luther finished second in his class of seventeen (Kittelson and Wiersma, *Luther the Reformer*, 12).

Section 1: The Legacy of Martin Luther and the Reformation

One month into law school, the twenty-one-year-old took a leave of absence from the faculty of law and visited his parents in the summer of 1505. As Luther returned to the university, he was caught in a thunderstorm near Stotternheim, just north of Erfurt. Flashes of lightning around him struck Luther to the ground. Immediately he cried out to the patron saint of miners, "Help me St. Anne! I will become a monk!" Upon hearing word of the monastic vow, Hans was furious, primarily because his investment in Martin for the future security of the Luder estate was now in jeopardy. After some deliberation, and much to his chagrin, Hans conceded to the wishes of young Luther, and Luther became a monk.

Luther demonstrated his willingness to pay the price of his convictions when, upon entering the monastery, he dispossessed himself of his beloved lute, though by this time he was a proficient musician, his costly *Corpus Juris Civilis*, and other material goods. Though Luther himself later regretted making the vow to St. Anne, he became an excellent monk: "If ever a monk could have reached heaven through monkery, then it was I."[7]

Luther joined the Augustinian cloister in Erfurt, an order that was known for its robust engagement in spiritual contemplation. As with his university education, Martin applied the same drive and disciplined work ethic that he had learned from childhood to his monastic vows. Within a year, Luther passed speedily from a guest of the Black Cloister, to novitiate, to priest celebrating his first Mass. Cognizant of the gravity of the task and rife with anxiety, Luther shook violently during his first Eucharist, almost dropping the bread and spilling the cup. These were the early signs of Luther's fear of God— a fear that would send him on a spiritual journey, a cross-examination of his soul to determine whether or not he were righteous before God.

Before long, the Augustinian friars recognized Luther for his spiritual battle with the soul. Now a priest, Luther took his monkery to a new level, depriving himself of food and water for days at a time, sleeping without the comfort of the allotted blanket, even flagellating himself. Luther did not merely go through the motions of denying self; he mortified the flesh with all vigor. So it was no wonder, when a dispute arose among various monastic orders in 1510, that the friars elected Luther to journey to Rome on their behalf. If anyone embodied the beliefs of the approximate three hundred monks of the Black Cloister and could adequately represent their position, it was Luther.

But Luther's expectations of drawing closer to God by visiting the Holy City which bore the divine name, ascending the *scala sancta* ("holy stairway"), walking in the footsteps of Saints Peter and Paul, and offering Mass in proximity to the Vicar of Christ were not met. Conversely, the visit to Rome sowed

---

7. Hendrix, "Legends about Luther," 48.

more seeds of doubt and fear in Luther's heart. What Luther saw appalled him—public urination, mindless observants conducting hurried Masses, and rampant prostitution for laity and priests alike. The center of Christendom was not the Eternal City Luther had envisioned. The impression it left on Luther can be summarized by his exclamation after he had ascended the holy stairway, pausing on each step to pray, in hopes of freeing his grandfather's soul from purgatory: "Who knows if it is really true?"[8]

Upon his return from Rome, Luther's *Anfechtung* intensified. Luther was riddled with fear of God and despaired of the Father's love for him. The spiritual temptations with which he did battle proved to be for Luther mightier than even the grace of God could overcome. Although elected to travel to Rome to represent the monastic brethren regarding a dispute within the Augustinian order, Luther's case was not even heard. Thus, the friars wanted to send him back. But by this time it was too late. Rome's lingering bitter taste forbade a second visit to Rome while his conscience on the divisive matter of the monks bid Luther leave the Black Cloister in Erfurt. Within short order, Luther was transferred to the monastery at Wittenberg.

These transformational years equipped Luther to become a stalwart leader through much adversity. His trivium education, particularly the skill of *argumentatio*, prepared Luther for his future stand-offs with emperors and papal theologians. He had learned how to think from Aristotle, speak from Seneca, and exegete a text from Cicero. Moreover, Luther's steadfast commitment to his convictions, even in the face of opposition and estrangement from his family, were the early signs of courage the leader would later need to commence and sustain a Reformation.[9] Finally, his willingness to spiritually cross-examine his soul regularly and battle his *Anfechtung* laid the foundation for Luther's discovery of justification by faith.

THE REFORMER'S CONVICTIONAL YEARS

Nearly a month after Luther's arrival in Wittenberg, Johann von Staupitz, dean of the theological faculty at the University of Wittenberg, pressured Luther to become a professor of theology and preacher at the town's Castle Church. Though Luther objected, "It will be the death of me!" his mentor Staupitz prevailed and within a year Luther had received his doctoral cap at the age

---

8. Oberman, "Fool in Rome," 47.

9. After celebrating his first Mass, Luther asked his father to reflect on his performance, to which Hans replied, "Have you not heard the commandment to honor your father and mother?" (Kittelson and Wiersma, *Luther the Reformer*, 20).

Section 1: The Legacy of Martin Luther and the Reformation

of twenty-nine.[10] Showing great promise, Dr. Martin rose within the ranks of the Augustinian friars at Wittenberg and was placed in charge of various duties which he executed with excellence. Speaking tongue-in-cheek, Luther once quipped, "You see how lazy I am," after he had recounted to a friend his responsibilities in Wittenberg as "a preacher at the monastery, a reader at meals . . . a parish preacher, director of studies, supervisor to eleven monasteries, superintendent of the fish pond at Litzkau, referee of a squabble at Torgau, lecturer on Paul, a collector of materials for the commentary on Psalms, and then, as I said, I am overwhelmed with letters."[11] Beyond this, Luther was still a professor, and lecture he did, exegeting the theological treatises of Psalms (1513–15), Romans (1515–16), Galatians (1516–17), Hebrews (1517–18), and returning a second time to Psalms (1518–21).

Amidst such busyness, Luther nonetheless found time to wrestle with his unrelenting conscience and the seeds of doubt planted in bygone years. What gnawed at Luther was the meaning of the righteousness of God: "For in it the righteousness of God is revealed from faith for faith, as it is written, 'The righteous shall live by faith.'" It was not the word *faith* that haunted Luther's soul, but the word *righteous*. Luther knew that his attempts at daily confession, penance, fasting, and prayers were insufficient to satisfy a righteous God. Through reading the works of Augustine against the Pelagians, a rigorous study of the current commentaries, and examining the original, biblical languages, Luther embarked on a journey to jettison late medieval theological teaching and redefine the meaning of God's righteousness. For Luther, God's righteousness was not merely the quality which the Divine Being possessed and by which he found humanity wanting, but it was a gift from God to humanity on account of Christ, a passive righteousness as Luther coined it:

> At last, as I meditated day and night on the relation of the words "the righteousness of God is revealed in it, as it is written, the righteous person shall live by faith," I began to understand that "righteousness of God" as that by which the righteous person lives by the gift of God; and this sentence, "the righteousness of God is revealed," to refer to a passive righteousness, by which the merciful God justifies us by faith, as it is written, "the righteous person lives by faith." This immediately made me feel as though I had been born again, and as though I had entered through open gates into paradise itself. From that moment, I saw the whole face of Scripture in a new light. . . . And now, where I had once hated the phrase, "the righteousness of God," I began to love and extol it

---

10. George, "Dr. Luther's Theology," 18.
11. *LW* 48:27–28.

> as the sweetest of phrases, so that this passage in Paul became the very gate of paradise to me.[12]

This breakthrough in thinking has since been codified as *sola fide* ("faith alone") and signifies a hallmark of Luther's theology, one of the five pillar contributions to the theological enterprise borne out of the Reformation.

Concurrently, Luther's view of Christ was evolving. The implications of *sola fide* meant that faith was not a residual virtue of a post-fall humanity that must be cultivated through the sacraments of Catholic medieval theology in order to work one's way toward salvation. For in that vein, salvation depended not on Christ's work on the cross, but on one's aptitude and capacity for faith as granted through obedience to the ritual sacraments. The rub for Luther was Romans 5: "Therefore, as one trespass led to condemnation for all men, so one act of righteousness leads to justification and life for all men. For as by the one man's disobedience the many were made sinners, so by the one man's obedience the many will be made righteous." For Luther, the "one act" of Christ on the cross and subsequent imputation of his righteousness to the sinner on the basis of faith led Luther to the *solo Christo* ("Christ alone") conclusion, the second pillar of his hallmark theology. Salvation from the "dark night of the soul" was not accomplished through human strivings. Rather, release from the unrelenting, burdened conscious is found in Christ alone:

> For if some complaint should be registered against a heart that believes in Christ, and testify against it concerning some evil deed, then the heart turns itself away, and turns to Christ, and says, "But he made satisfaction. He is the righteous one, and this is my defense. He died for me, he made his righteousness mine and made my sin his own; and if he made my sin his own, then I do not have it, and I am free."[13]

Therefore, it is incumbent upon the sinner to place complete faith in Christ and not base one's standing before God on his own merits of goodwill.

> Therefore, my sweet brother, learn Christ and him crucified; despairing of yourself, learn to pray him, saying, "You Lord Jesus, are my righteousness, but I am your sin; you have taken on yourself what you were not and have given me what I was not." Beware of aspiring to such purity that you no longer wish to appear to yourself, or to be, a sinner.[14]

---

12. George, "Dr. Luther's Theology," 20.
13. *LW* 25:188.
14. *LW* 48:12–13.

Section 1: The Legacy of Martin Luther and the Reformation

These revolutionary ideas of *sola fide* and *solo Christo* cut against the grain of the selling of indulgences. Indulgences were certificates promising to expedite a soul's transfer from Purgatory to Paradise. Whereas the soul might have to spend years in Purgatory having the residual dross of the postmortem sinful nature purged, the purchase of an indulgence by a loved one still living could shave off years of the soul's purging and position him in the Divine presence sooner than expected. So, when Johann Tetzel came near Wittenberg by decree of the Bishop of Rome marketing indulgences with his slogan, "As soon as the coin in the coffer rings, the soul from purgatory heavenward springs," Luther was incensed. While stewing over Tetzel's abuse of indulgences, which amounted to racketeering in order to finance the building of St. Peter's Basilica in Rome, Luther took up a prophetic quill and penned 95 *Theses* of protestations against the papal practice. Luther nailed his *Disputatio pro Declaratione Virtutis Indulgentiarum* to the Castle Church door on October 31, 1517, challenging Tetzel and others in the region to debate the merits of indulgences. Luther lit the match on that fateful day; unbeknownst to him, Europe was a tinderbox.

The convictional years of Luther brought with them a heightened sensitivity to the discipline with which one ought to study the Bible and the accuracy with which one ought to teach God's Word. Through scrupulous study of the Scripture, Luther made inroads to better understanding the roles of faith and Christ in the salvific process. Luther's two-pronged *sola* discovery, however, stood at odds with the common practices of late medieval Roman Catholicism and positioned him at a crossroads. But the Reformation leader was poised for action. Luther made the plunge to take a stance on his understanding of what the Scriptures taught, even if it meant defying Rome. Soon he would discover that he stood alone.

THE REFORMER'S DEFIANT YEARS

Within two weeks the doctor's 95 *Theses* spread throughout Germany and within six months, all of Europe knew the friar's name. Luther had not intended that his theses circulate so far and wide, but the invention of the Gutenberg Press made Luther a viral sensation. While his theses emboldened the peasants, they enraged the pope. Luther's publication drew lines in the sand and forced a showdown between himself and the papacy. A year after their publication, Luther was summoned to the Diet of Augsburg, not to dispute indulgences as had been his initial invitation in the theses, but to recant. For the Vicar of Rome, the *Disputatio* was an attack on his authority and Luther had to be brought back into submission.

Cardinal Cajetan, the vicar-general of the Dominicans, presided over the meetings and was given authority to declare Luther a "notorious heretic" if he did not utter *revoco* ("I recant"). Though the Diet began cordially, its continuation over several days turned to a most heated debate. Cajetan sought to have Luther reject his teaching that the pope lacked the merits to issue indulgences and that faith was the basis for justification, while further commanding Luther never to teach such things again nor stir up further trouble in the church. Luther retorted that the selling of indulgences was a Ponzi scheme, that faith was necessary to make the sacraments effective, and that the doctrines of the councils of men were above the *Bulla* of the popes.[15] Turning as red as his cardinal robes, Catejan threatened to condemn Luther and excommunicate his friends. But the stubborn monk would not budge. From Luther's perspective, there was nothing that he needed to recant since his teachings were based on God's Word. When Luther then appealed to have his case heard at Rome, Catejan faced an impasse. His mission to secure one simple word from the Augustinian friar failed—*revoco* was not in Luther's vocabulary.

Where Catejan failed, Johann Eck of Ingolstadt would succeed—or so he thought. Eck challenged Luther and his fellow Wittenbergers to a debate at Leipzig the following summer. If Catejan's debate turned heated, Eck's started in a furnace. Two hundred Wittenberg students armed with "pikes and staves for the sake of security" accompanied Luther, while Eck's seventy-five men brandishing weapons lined the debate chamber of Castle Pleissenburg.[16] The ten-day debate narrowed its focus to a central question: Who holds ultimate authority over the church? For Eck, it was the pope who holds the "Keys of Heaven," which he defended from Jesus's response to Peter's confession in Matthew 16. For Luther, it was Christ, because popes are fallible and even councils err by condemning innocent men as heretics (e.g., Jan Hus). Consequently, Luther explained that the Scriptures dictate the doctrines of men, not vice versa: "A simple layman armed with Scripture is to be believed above a pope or a council without it. . . . Neither the Church nor the pope can establish articles of faith. These must come from Scripture. For the sake of Scripture we should reject pope and councils."[17]

With this Luther laid the foundation for a third pillar of Reformation theology, *sola Scriptura* ("Scripture alone"). The medieval theology of the Catholic Church taught that the traditions of men and decrees of the pope carried the same weight as that of Scripture itself. But Luther saw the church as begotten from the Bible, and therefore the church has no right to exercise

---

15. Kittelson and Wiersma, *Luther the Reformer*, 86.
16. Ibid., 100–101.
17. Bainton, *Here I Stand*, 90.

Section 1: The Legacy of Martin Luther and the Reformation

authority over the Word of God.[18] The Bible alone holds supreme authority in matters of faith and practice—all else is suspect: "What is asserted without the Scriptures or proven revelation may be held as an opinion, but need not be believed."[19]

The conviction of *sola Scriptura* sustained Luther the following year when Pope Leo X issued *Exurge Domine* giving Luther sixty days to recant or face excommunication. In response, Luther burned the papal bull and penned three important treatises, setting him at odds with most all teaching of Catholic Christendom. In one of those treatises, *The Address to the Christian Nobility*, Luther expounded a fourth hallmark of his theology—the priesthood of the believer:

> How then if they are forced to admit that we are all equally priests, as many of us as are baptized, and by this way we truly are; while to them is committed only the Ministry (ministerium Predigtamt) and consented to by us (nostro consensu)? If they recognize this they would know that they have no right to exercise power over us (ius imperii in what has not been committed to them) except insofar as we may have granted it to them, for thus it says in 1 Peter 2, "You are a chosen race, a royal priesthood, a priestly kingdom." In this way we are all priests, as many of us as are Christians. There are indeed priests whom we call ministers. They are chosen from among us, and who do everything in our name. That is a priesthood which is nothing else than the Ministry. Thus 1 Corinthians 4:1: "No one should regard us as anything else than ministers of Christ and dispensers of the mysteries of God."[20]

Taking his cue from Scripture, Luther advocated the "greatest contribution to Protestant ecclesiology."[21] He understood that Christianity is not meant to be lived out in isolation but that "every Christian is someone else's priest; and we are all priests to one another."[22] Thus, there are no super-Christians like the papacy purported, nor a caste of holy men privileged to the priestly office. Rather, the priesthood is the prerogative of all Christians. With this revolutionary teaching, Luther leveled the playing field and bridged the divide which separated laity from clergy.

Armed with the Scriptures and emboldened by his discovery of the true priesthood, Luther departed with the summons in hand for the Diet of Worms

18. George, "Dr. Luther's Theology," 19.
19. Ibid.
20. *LW* 36:112–13.
21. George, *Theology of the Reformers*, 95.
22. Ibid., 96.

in the spring 1521. What he encountered at Worms was not what he expected. On the one hand, Luther was greeted by trumpeters announcing his arrival. Two thousand peasants, princes, and politicians lined the streets to catch a glimpse of the doctor. The debate hall was filled with Germany's powerful echelon of princes and bishops. Even the newly elected Holy Roman Emperor Charles V (Charles I of Spain) was among the venerable guests. Girolamo Aleandro, a cross-examiner of Luther, remarked privately to his superiors, "Nine-tenths of the people are shouting 'Luther!' and the other tenth are crying 'Death to the Roman Court!'"[23] Luther was taken aback by the fanfare. Was this the evidence of a Reformation juggernaut? Or was it his Palm Sunday? On the other hand, Luther once again would not receive the debate he had hoped his summons implied. As Luther walked into the ecclesial hall, the examiner pointed to a pile of books in the middle of floor which had been written by Luther and asked him if he would recant of their teachings. Under duress, Luther prayed leave one day to consider his response, since "this touches God and his Word. This affects the salvation of souls. . . . To say too little or too much would be dangerous."[24] Dangerous indeed! Luther had two choices. He could recant of his teachings, thereby denying his convictions about Scripture. Or he could stand firm, even if it meant that the "Saxon Hus" might suffer the same fate as his Czechian predecessor.[25] The next day Luther returned emboldened, even more convinced of his convictions than ever before:

> Unless I can be instructed and convinced with evidence from the Holy Scriptures or with open, clear, and distinct grounds and reasoning—and my conscience is captive to the Word of God—then I cannot and will not recant, because it is neither safe nor wise to act against conscience.[26]

Finally, Luther concluded, "Here I stand; I can do no other. May God help me. Amen."[27] The next day the Emperor ruled *contra* Luther calling him a heretic and promising to wield his power against Luther to ban him from the empire.

---

23. Thigpen, "Gallery of Friends and Enemies," 41.

24. Bainton, *Here I Stand*, 141.

25. Jan Hus was the Reformer of Prague who was deemed a heretic and burned at the stake in 1415. It is rumored that at his death, he prophesied, "This day ye roast a goose, but a hundred years hence a white swan will come, which ye will never be able to put to death." Nearly a hundred years after the death of Hus, Luther nailed his 95 *Theses* to the Castle Church door in Wittenberg. Since Luther's convictions aligned closely with those of Hus, Luther earned the nickname the "Saxon Hus" (Lenfant, *History of the Council of Constance*, 447).

26. *LW* 32:105–31.

27. Kittelson and Wiersma, *Luther the Reformer*, 121.

Section 1: The Legacy of Martin Luther and the Reformation

Still, Charles V granted Luther twenty-one days of safe passage back to Wittenberg before his protection expired. But Luther never made it home.

Frederick III, "the Wise" Elector of Saxony, founder of the University of Wittenberg, and financier of Luther's doctorate, secured his investment by having Luther kidnapped en route from Worms to Wittenberg. Under the auspices of Frederick the Wise, "Prince George," as Luther was now called, lived incognito in the fortified castle at Wartburg. Over the course of eleven months, Luther devoured Erasmus of Rotterdam's Greek and Latin New Testaments translating them into the vernacular German at a breakneck speed of 1,500 words per day.[28] *Das Newe Testament Deutzsch*, his crowning achievement, was published in the winter 1522 with three thousand printed copies circulating Germany.[29] The *Lutherbibel* became a common household book. Its eloquence and ease of reading ensured its presence on the tongues of every German, from peasant to prince.[30] Luther had left an indelible mark; his leadership of the German Reformation was eternally etched on the hearts of men for the Word of God he left in their hand.

THE REFORMER'S FAMILY YEARS

Having stood against pope and emperor and prevailed, what challenge could the defiant monk tackle next that might compare? Starting a family! During the 1518 Diet of Augsburg, Staupitz, fearing the outcome of the debate with Catejan, had secretly released Luther from his monastic vows.[31] After Luther emerged from his eleven-month hiding in the Wartburg Castle, he acted upon that liberty to marry. Luther returned to Wittenberg and in 1525 the forty-one-year-old rebel monk sought the hand of the runaway nun Katharina von Bora, sixteen years his junior. Luther met Katie when he undertook the responsibility of playing matchmaker for a group of twelve runaway nuns. He found suitors for most of the women, but for Katie, none was sufficient.[32] So Luther married her himself, much to the delight of his father Hans.

Having been a monk for twenty years, marriage would indeed present changes, challenges, and lifestyle adjustments. For one, Luther marveled at the fact that now meals were eaten in the company of another.[33] The strangest

28. Jacobsen, "Martin Luther's Early Years," 2.
29. Brown, "Preaching," 34.
30. Zecher, "Bible Translation," 37.
31. Kittelson and Wiersma, *Luther the Reformer*, 87.
32. Thigpen, "Gallery—Family Album," 14.
33. Kittelson and Wiersma, *Luther the Reformer*, 161.

thing about married life for Luther was waking up and seeing Katie's pigtails on the pillow next to him.[34] Though Martin did not marry out of love, he learned to love and cherish Katherine, affectionately dubbing her his "Eve," or at times wryly calling her "my lord Kate."[35] Their love for one another brought about another change—the introduction of children. The Luthers were fruitful . . . and fast. Four months into their marriage union, Luther announced, "My Katherine is fulfilling Genesis 1:28."[36] In the wake of their firstborn son Hans (1526), five more children followed in rapid succession: Elizabeth (1527), Magdalena (1529), Martin (1531), Paul (1533), and finally Margaret (1534). Luther's care for his family was evident, and even though he referred to the children as his "little heathens," he took seriously his role as shepherd of this little flock. For it was during these years that Luther set about writing *The Small Catechism* and *The Large Catechism*; the former explains the faith to children and the latter expounds the biblical doctrines to the laity.

The Luther family lived in the Black Cloister of Wittenberg, the monastery bequeathed to them as a wedding gift from the Electorate of Saxony.[37] The *Lutherhaus* was a half-home, half-hostel and accommodated as many as thirty guests at a time, whether university students, orphans, monks and nuns, or the poor and sick. The Luthers showed great charity to others, even admitting a victim of the Peasants' War into their home on the night of their wedding and converting the house to an infirmary while a plague-ravaged Wittenberg.[38] Due to Martin's frequent travels during these years, Katie became a superb manager of the estate, to the extent that Luther once remarked, "In domestic affairs I defer to Katie. Otherwise, I am led by the Holy Ghost."[39] At any given time she could be found planting the fields, harvesting the orchard, tending the brewery, or slaughtering the livestock.[40]

These family years brought on a different leadership role for Luther. In his early years, the defiant monk's stance on his convictions precipitated the Reformation. Now the aged theologian had to flesh out those convictions in a way that proved their sustainability of the Reformation. As Luther began articulating the implications of this Reformation, no sector of society remained resilient from its intended transformation by Luther's quill. From the political sphere to the educational system, all received a proposed facelift from Luther.

34. Galli, "Monk Marries," 24; *LW* 54:191.
35. Kittelson and Wiersma, *Luther the Reformer*, 162.
36. Thigpen, "Gallery—Family Album," 15.
37. Ozment, "Reinventing Family Life," 25.
38. Galli, "Did You Know?," 3.
39. Galli, "Monk Marries," 24.
40. Thigpen, "Gallery—Family Album," 15.

Section 1: The Legacy of Martin Luther and the Reformation

But it was the church which particularly had Luther's interest and so he set about revising its liturgy. He wanted the laypeople to benefit from the worship experience by conducting the Mass in a language they understood. Thus, Latin was replaced by German. Luther produced the *German Mass and Order of Divine Service* and gave the fledgling Protestant movement a unique interpretation of the Lord's Supper, promoting *consubstantiation* (Christ's presence alongside the bread/wine) over against medieval Catholic teaching of *transubstantiation* (bread/wine become Christ's presence) and Zwinglian *spiritual presence* (bread/wine symbol of Christ's presence). Luther commissioned artists and musicians to write new, German hymns primarily from the Psalms and introduced congregational singing. Being a gifted musician himself, the hymnodist contributed to the cause and composed some forty songs, one of which is the famed *A Mighty Fortress Is Our God*. Moreover, he supplied the laity with a completed Bible in the vernacular, having translated the Old Testament by 1534. Through the precise, methodical hand of friend and colleague Philipp Melanchthon, Luther codified his beliefs in the *Augsburg Confession*—a statement of faith outlining the essentials of Christian doctrine and liturgy for the new church. Luther's supporters embraced these changes and more reforms laying the foundation for the Lutheran denomination which followed.

Among these church reforms, Luther had yet a fifth and final hallmark of theology to contribute to the Reformation—*sola gratia* ("grace alone"). Luther published his *On the Bondage of the Will* a year after Erasmus's *On Freedom of the Will*. The tit-for-tat treatises addressed the critical facets of salvation, specifically predestination, free will, and of course grace. Luther's *sola fide* had already revolutionized medieval thinking on salvation. But his *sola gratia* would remove human contribution from the center of salvation in the same way Copernicus removed the earth from the center of the universe.[41] In both cases, the Son/sun would take center stage. Luther believed that the human condition was enslaved to sin and therefore had no capacity for faith: "*Grace puts God in the place of everything else it sees, and prefers him to itself, but [the fallen human will] puts itself in the place of everything, and even in the place of God, and seeks only its own and not what is God's.*"[42] If faith in God is not a human possibility, concluded Luther, then it too must be a gift from the Divine Being. Therefore, salvation from beginning to end is an act of grace, and grace alone.

---

41. George, "Dr. Luther's Theology," 20.

42. Rup and Watson, *Luther and Erasmus*, 220, as quoted in George, *Theology of the Reformers*, 75.

THE REFORMER'S FINAL YEAR

In an era when the life expectancy hovered around forty, it is nothing short of remarkable that Luther lived to be sixty-two years old, having endured all manner of sickness, to say nothing of the toll taken on his body from the anxiety and stress which came from standing firm and alone before princes and popes alike.[43] Yet despite Luther's failing health and bouts of depression that year, he traveled to Eisleben, the city of his birth, to settle a mining dispute between three counts of Mansfield in 1546. Having successfully arbitrated among the factitious brothers, Luther concluded his business in Eisleben with a sermon from Matthew 11:25–30 calling all to come and submit to Christ. But Luther abruptly ended the sermon. Overcome by weakness, he departed to his bed chambers from which he never emerged. Within a few days he died on February 18. In the final hours of his life, Luther scribbled on a piece of paper, "We are beggars. This is true."[44] His life's work and heart's final posture embodied the Reformers' foundational belief, *soli Deo gloria*.

---

43. Edwards, "After the Revolution," 3, reports that Luther "suffered from constipation, diarrhea, hemorrhoids, dizziness, ringing in his ears, an ulcer on his leg, kidney stones, and heart problems."

44. *LW* 54:476.

2

Faith, Scripture, and Vocation
The Spiritual Legacies of Martin Luther on Protestant Evangelicalism

Dr. Michael Whiting

Salvation by faith in Christ alone apart from works, the translation of the Bible to be read in vernacular languages by all people as the supreme authority of Christian faith and practice, and the sanctity of all clerical and lay vocations and callings in the world—these are values celebrated by Protestant evangelicals today that it would seem incredible that they were not always believed or shared by others in the history of the Christian tradition.[1] In fact, at one point in time, they were among the most controversial values that in the

---

1. By Protestant evangelicalism, I am referring to those Christian traditions as heirs of the Reformation that stress the supreme authority of the Scriptures and a transforming, personal salvific relationship with God through faith alone in Jesus Christ. The standard definition of eighteenth-century "evangelicalism" remains that of David Bebbington who identified four distinguishing characteristics: the Bible as authority; the cross of Christ as central in redemption; the necessity of a personal conversion experience; and the expression of faith in mission witness and social activism. See, e.g., Bebbington, "Evangelicals of the World," 21–51. Although differing in some respects from later British and American evangelicalism, the spiritual legacies of Luther that will be described in this chapter overlap significantly with Bebbington's definition and demonstrate modern evangelicalism's fundamental indebtedness to the reforms of Luther. See also MacKenzie, "Evangelical Character," 171–98.

1500s contributed to the unstoppable rupture of the Catholic Church and the radical transformation of European culture.

Behind these values that literally transformed the way people thought about being Christian lies the influence of Martin Luther, an Augustinian friar virtually unknown before 1517 but whose reforming activities would take a rather obscure town like Wittenberg, Saxony, and transform it into a leading center of religious, social, cultural, political, and even economic development.[2] Luther's rise to popularity and influence is rather a startling story and would have surprised his contemporaries, who hardly could have believed that this one Augustinian friar would be the subject of so much attention five hundred years later. After all, it was not the first time that the Catholic Church had to deal with a dissenting voice calling for reform. What made this Augustinian friar's influence so explosive? Perhaps it was the degree to which Luther sought a complete theological revolution in the Church, challenging even the most fundamental beliefs and practices long held by the medieval Catholic tradition. Perhaps it was the degree to which the Roman papacy had declined in its prestige and power in the late medieval world. The papacy had grown so strong by the thirteenth century under Innocent III as to dictate policy to foreign kings and emperors threatening them with the divine powers of excommunication. Yet corruption of popes and schisms in the papacy—at one time two or three popes vying for power and for almost forty years a pope in Rome and a pope in France—weakened the prestige of the papacy and its claims of authority over the religious and political affairs of foreign nations. Maybe Luther came at a time when many nationalistic-minded princes in Germany were ready to rid themselves of subjection to a foreign pope and his alignment with a domineering emperor. Furthermore, unlike Reformers of earlier centuries, Luther had the technological advantage of the printing press that spread his writings and ideas at a rate beyond effective papal and episcopal control.

However much Luther's impact is interpreted with regard to these and other sociopolitical factors, this little monk was able to inspire an explosive, variegated movement that would radically transform German culture and beyond. It was never Luther's plan or intent to begin a Lutheran denomination, and it is not only Lutherans who have inherited and benefited from the spiritual legacy of his theological revolution.

The purpose of this chapter is to develop the impact of Luther on the formation of the distinctive spiritual heritage of Protestant evangelicalism as a whole, especially its emphasis on the common priesthood of believers through faith in Jesus Christ. This idea was rooted in Luther's reformed understanding of justification (by faith alone, Christ alone, grace alone, to the glory of God

2. Pettegree, *Brand Luther*. For Luther's biography, see Mullett, *Martin Luther*.

Section 1: The Legacy of Martin Luther and the Reformation

alone) and was defended on the basis of his reading and interpretation of the Bible (Scripture alone). The priesthood of believers not only impacted how people viewed assurance of their salvation but how they understood the value of their vocations and callings in the world. However, this doctrine would have meant less without its practical implementation and realization through the translation of the Bible to be read by the common people. Scriptural translation is a major factor in the incredible spread of Christianity in the last century in the "majority world" among peoples of Asia, Africa, and Latin America. Luther's theology of justification by faith alone and the common priesthood of believers left an indelible spiritual legacy on the future of Protestant evangelicalism by empowering all believers with a more intimate, accessible relationship with God through faith in Jesus Christ and reading of his Word while dignifying their various callings of service to others in the world.

THE FOUNDATION: LUTHER'S NEW PERSPECTIVES ON SALVATION

By the end of the Middle Ages, the Roman Catholic Church had developed a rather complex system of salvation from baptism as an infant to the grave that privileged the sacramental powers of the clergy, or sacerdotalism, leaving the commoners more helpless, dependent, and passive in their relationship with God. The clergy were the gatekeepers of access to God, claiming an authoritative monopoly over the interpretation of divine things and controlling the administration of forgiveness and reconciliation through the sacrament of confession, or penance, and the granting of indulgences. No one could appear before the Lord in heaven without perfect holiness, and it was through personal penitence, piety, and the sacramental rites of the church that baptized Christians hoped to be made righteous and attain the vision of God. While condemnation to hell was reserved for the most wicked and unbelieving, most baptized Christians expected to spend several thousand years in purgatory to be disciplined and purged of the remaining sinful dross that clung to their fallen natures. Pious Christians also venerated saints' images and relics, went on pilgrimages to holy shrines and churches, and paid for special Masses with the hope of shaving off some years in purgatory for themselves or a loved one already on the postmortem journey.

If you really wanted to get serious about religion and God during this period, the most dedicated Christians in the Middle Ages entered the monastic life. After all, a monk had left the pleasures of the world behind to pursue union with God through fasting, chastity, and devotion to prayer. The vice of greed was subdued by sharing all things in common with the brothers (or in the case of convents, with sisters). The vice of lust was repressed by vows of celibacy and singular dedication to heavenly things. The vice of ambition or pride was choked by vows of humility and submission to one another and, ultimately, the abbot.

It was such a mindset that prompted Luther to enter the Augustinian Cloister in Erfurt in 1505. He was merely following what the Church had taught, that a monastic life of voluntary sacrifice and suffering was the most serious and dedicated Christian life, the life most in conformity with Christ, and thus, the one most assured to ease the path toward the enjoyment of heavenly glory.

However, rather than increasing in assurance with God, Luther developed a hateful distrust of God. His demands were simply too high to achieve, even for a devout monk like Luther who far surpassed his brothers in rigorous fasting and confession. It was in this context of doubting and the dark night of his soul that Luther arrived at a new conclusion about justification before God. While lecturing at the University of Wittenberg on the book of Romans in 1515–16, and while also reading the anti-Pelagian works of St. Augustine, Luther came to understand that access to God was not achieved through striving to do more and more works of righteousness as he had been trained to believe but in passively receiving God's righteousness as a total gift through faith in Jesus Christ. Salvation is by faith alone, grace alone, through Christ alone, to the glory of God alone.

In his *Disputation Against Scholastic Theology* (1517), Luther attacks Aristotle's philosophy as having negatively influenced medieval interpretations of virtue and righteousness, arguing that the natural sin nature and the law of God are at enmity with one another. The natural will bent on sin wishes that God and the law would not exist. Thus, works that are extracted with hesitation, by compulsion, or even for hope of personal reward are not truly good works and do not deserve to be considered as meritorious for justification before God. Contrary to natural thinking, the discipline of striving to build habits of virtue does not make one virtuous in the sight of God. That is to put the cart before the horse, or in Luther's analogy the apple before the tree. Righteousness is the fruit of a preceding spiritual change wrought by the gospel. The following theses illustrate this point:

> 17. Man is by nature unable to want God to be God. Indeed, he himself wants to be God, and does not want God to be God.[3]

---

3. *LW* 31:10.

Section 1: The Legacy of Martin Luther and the Reformation

> 40. We do not become righteous by doing righteous deeds but, having been made righteous, we do righteous deeds. This in opposition to the philosophers.[4]
>
> 71. Law and will are two implacable foes without the grace of God.[5]
>
> 85. Anyone's will would prefer, if it were possible, that there would be no law and to be entirely free.[6]

In articles prepared for a meeting of the Augustinians Order in Heidelberg (1518), Luther contrasts the theology of glory that places the onus on man to live up to God's demands with the theology of the cross, which reveals just how far man is depraved that God would have to come to his rescue through the suffering, humiliation, and death of the righteous Son of God. The law makes its demands but provides no strength to fulfill it. The gospel says to believe that what the law has demanded Christ has fulfilled on behalf of man. Thus, as Luther states in thesis 25: "He is not righteous who does much, but he who, without work, believes much in Christ."[7]

Accusations that such a theology would endorse lawlessness and immorality were responded to by Luther by his emphasis that faith is the living work of the Holy Spirit that produces good works and submits the sinful nature to the instruction and correction of the law of God. Faith brings the joy and love of the Holy Spirit and the strength to do truly good works from the heart, not to merit God's eternal favor received through faith in Christ alone, but to bring glory to God, to keep the sinful nature in check, and to serve the needs of the neighbor.

The doctrine of justification by faith alone and the proper distinction between law and gospel became major themes in Luther's pastoral writings, treatises, and sermons, beginning with such important works as his *Treatise on Good Works* and *Freedom of a Christian* in 1520. The former exposits the Ten Commandments as the wisdom of God concerning his will for man with faith as the fulfillment of the First Commandment and the fountain of all the rest that flow from it. The latter treatise discusses the double truth that justification is a total reliance upon God's grace in Christ Jesus by faith alone apart from works on the one hand but that such faith by the Spirit is also alive and active in driving out sins and doing good works for others, even though such works do not justify or make one righteous before God.

---

4. *LW* 31:12.
5. *LW* 31:14.
6. *LW* 31:15; see also Luther's, *Bondage of the Will* (1525), *LW* 33.
7. *LW* 31:41.

> Just as our neighbor is in need and lacks that in which we abound, so we were in need before God and lacked his mercy. Hence, as our heavenly Father has in Christ freely come to our aid, we also ought freely to help our neighbor through our body and its works, and each one should become as it were a Christ to the other that we may be Christs to one another and Christ may be the same in all, that is, that we may be truly Christians.[8]

Luther's theology of salvation by faith alone radically transformed how people in late medieval / early modern Germany understood their relationship to God. No longer was it necessary to privately confess mortal sins to a priest to be reconciled to God (although Luther would continue to encourage the counseling benefits of confession). The monastic life was no longer the surest path to heaven. In fact, it fostered a theology of works righteousness that kept people in slavery to the law under the condemnation of God. Thus, medieval sacerdotalism, which elevated the superiority of the priesthood and monastic life in closer proximity to God, was leveled so that the differences between clergy and laity, for Luther, are simply ones of office and calling, not of righteous status, meritorious virtue, or spiritual worth before God. Luther states in his *Address to the Christian Nobility* in 1520 that all Christians are, in fact, consecrated equally as priests by virtue of their one baptism into the faith and gospel of Jesus Christ.[9]

The intercession of Mary and other saints to implore Christ on man's behalf was likewise unnecessary since all are sinners and come to Christ on equal ground. Penances, fasts, pilgrimages, indulgences, and Masses do not contribute to any merit for eternal life for the living or the dead. Purgatory was a false idea since entrance to heaven is not by man's righteousness but by faith in Christ's alien righteousness. One can see the radical impact that such an idea had on transforming a whole religious worldview and empowering the common people with a greater sense of their own direct, personal access to Christ and to the Father. This is a defining characteristic of Protestant evangelicalism even today, especially given the emphasis in the modern Western world on the value and dignity of the individual.

---

8. *LW* 31:367–68.
9. *LW* 44:128–29.

Section 1: The Legacy of Martin Luther and the Reformation

THE IMPLEMENTATION: LUTHER'S NEW PERSPECTIVES ON SCRIPTURE AND RELIGIOUS INSTRUCTION OF THE PEOPLE

The foundation of Luther's revolutionary theology was the authority of the Scriptures that communicate the reliable testimony concerning the Word of God, the gospel of Jesus Christ. As he states in his *Freedom of a Christian*:

> The Word is the gospel of God concerning his Son, who was made flesh, suffered, rose from the dead, and was glorified through the Spirit who sanctifies. To preach Christ means to feed the soul, make it righteous, set it free, and save it, provided it believes the preaching.... The Word of God cannot be received and cherished by any works whatever but only by faith. Therefore it is clear that, as the soul needs only the Word of God for its life and righteousness, so it is justified by faith alone and not any works; for if it could be justified by anything else, it would not need the Word, and consequently it would not need faith.[10]

Late medieval practices and beliefs were contrary to the biblical gospel of justification by faith as Luther understood it, but they were also nowhere to be found as commandments in Scripture. This does not mean that Luther did away with every tradition that he could not find prescribed in Scripture. Thus, Lutheran churches used organs for musical worship while churches in Reformed Zurich did not. Luther was also more moderate toward images used for remembrance than his more iconoclastic Reformed contemporaries. Of all the Protestant Reformation churches, Lutheran (and Anglican) churches most resemble Catholic churches in the structure of their liturgy and the appearance of the sanctuary. For Luther, not all traditions fundamentally contradicted the gospel and needed to be discarded.

Luther's Reformation was fundamentally a matter of biblical interpretation, chiefly with respect to the gospel. For Reformers like Luther, the Scripture holds supreme authority for faith and practice. It alone binds consciences with the authority of God. This is also a critical characteristic of Protestant evangelicalism today. Emphasis on the supreme authority of the Bible sets Protestants apart from the Catholic and Orthodox Church. Protestants may often treat certain traditions, confessions of faith, and prominent pastors as equal in authority to Scripture, but this is more accidental than theoretical or foundational. The Catholic Church, however, does claim that a spiritual authority to dictate faith and practice, by their succession to the inspired

---

10. *LW* 31:346.

apostles, also resides in the ordained leadership of the Church, especially the papacy. For the Orthodox, they emphasize the Seven Ecumenical Councils and the traditions of the church's liturgy as authoritative with Scripture.

Luther's emphasis on the supreme authority of Scripture alone was certainly developed during his own lectures on the Bible, especially as he was framing a theology of justification at odds with his late medieval training in the Catholic tradition. Nevertheless, there were already movements in the Late Middle Ages that sought to bring greater attention to the Scriptures. Dissidents like John Wyclif in England and John Hus in Bohemia challenged many of the Roman Church's teachings and practices and chastised its leaders on the basis of Scripture. Philosophers such as William of Ockham emphasized scriptural revelation rather than logical speculation. A movement associated with the Renaissance placed greater emphasis on the rooting of Christian faith and piety in the knowledge of Scripture. Northern Renaissance humanist scholars cried *ad fontes* ("to the sources") in their desire to bring about educational reform leading to moral reformation in the Church. Thus, the Catholic humanist Erasmus of Rotterdam sought to motivate reform by revising the Latin translation of the New Testament, which he based off of the best manuscripts he could pull together of the Greek text. His publication of the Greek New Testament in 1516, the first of its kind in Europe and followed by further revised editions, would be a major tool used by Protestant Reformers in their more thorough reformation of the Church's theology argued on the basis of the Bible in its original languages.

It was not Luther's theology of justification by faith that initially brought the ire of Catholic authorities down upon his head. Rather, it was his *95 Theses* posted in 1517, subsequently translated and printed into German, that brought the issue of authority to the forefront. Luther intended the theses for academic debate as a good university scholar and doctor of theology was encouraged to do, but his attack on the sale of indulgences was an attack on the archbishop and also the papacy that authorized them to help with the rebuilding of St. Peter's basilica. Following the growing interest in Germany surrounding Luther's attack on indulgences (and the Roman papacy), Luther was summoned to Augsburg in 1518 to recant at a meeting with the papal legate, Cardinal Cajetan, but Luther refused unless his errors could be proven by Scripture. The powers that be were not interested in a biblical discussion about a common church tradition but in his submission and respect for authority. In 1519, he debated John Eck of Ingolstadt. During the debate, the issue of John Hus' burning at the stake for heresy in 1415 came up. Eck challenged Luther on whether the Council of Constance had made a mistake in condemning Hus. Luther replied that popes and councils can and have erred. Only the

Section 1: The Legacy of Martin Luther and the Reformation

written Scriptures are infallible and trustworthy. Then, following his excommunication in 1520, Luther appeared before Emperor Charles V at the Diet of Worms in 1521, giving his now famous "Here I Stand" speech and in which he declared his conscience as "captive to the Word of God."[11]

Thus, Luther's Reformation was defended on the basis of the supreme authority of Scripture alone in so far as he interpreted it. Luther did not intend to start a new denomination (and certainly not one called "Lutheran") or to break from the Catholic Church. He was willing to subject himself to the Catholic Church only if they could demonstrate that they based the authority of their own teachings on the clear and trustworthy testimony of the Scriptures. The Catholic Church and the Empire subsequently condemned him as an outlaw, thereby making the Reformation a movement officially outside the established State-Church.

Luther's many theological publications were translated into vernacular German to be read by all literate Christian Germans not just by the clergy and academics, thus bringing the light of the gospel to the common person, but his most important work was his translation of the New Testament (1522), and eventually the whole Bible (1534), into German. Luther states in his *Address to the Christian Nobility of the German Nation* in 1520 that the papacy had built up impenetrable walls that kept it from heeding necessary calls to reform, one of which was the claim that only popes could interpret Scripture.

> If it were to happen that the pope and his cohorts were wicked and not true Christians, were not taught by God and were without understanding, and at the same time some obscure person had a right understanding, why should the people not follow the obscure man? Has the pope not erred many times? Who would help Christendom when the pope erred if we did not have somebody we could trust more than him, somebody who had the Scriptures on his side?[12]

Consequently, Luther translated the New Testament while hiding out in the Wartburg Castle in 1522, utilizing Erasmus's recently revised Latin and Greek New Testament. It was his desire that the people could read the gospel in the Scriptures for themselves and no longer be enslaved to the errors of the Roman clergy if they simply had the Scriptures in their own hands and hearts. After all, this is what the Scriptures had done for him: "By translating the Scriptures he would not only be giving his people access to the source from

---

11. *LW* 32: 112–13.
12. *LW* 44:126, 134.

which he himself was drawing, he would also be justifying on a grand scale the direction in which he had so far been moving."[13]

To help reorient the German people in their transition to this new interpretation of the Scriptures, especially the gospel, Luther also wrote many prologues and prefaces to accompany his biblical translation, emphasizing knowledge of sin through the law and the central gospel theme of justification by faith alone in Christ. Luther also published sermon aids (*Postils*) for the new evangelical pastors and later revised the church's liturgy into German in 1525. His Large and Small Catechisms of 1529–30, structured according to the Ten Commandments, the Apostles' Creed, and the Lord's Prayer, were also an important vernacular literature of the German Reformation intended to guide instruction in the new evangelical faith within the churches and among families.

Luther's German Bible shaped the unity of the German language much like the King James Version did for the English language in the 1600s. This emphasis on the reading of the Scriptures in vernacular languages was a principal part of the Reformation given that the authority of God resides in the inspired text itself. This was another attack on sacerdotalism by emphasizing the common priesthood of believers as it relates to the reading and interpretation of Scripture. This did not mean that certain people were not called to teach and preach, but there was a confidence among the Protestant Reformers that the essentials of Scripture regarding what is necessary for salvation were clear and that the Scriptures should be made available for all Christians for reading and meditation as spiritual food for their sanctification.

The reading of Scripture by all Christians for personal devotion and spiritual benefit is among the primary spiritual legacies bequeathed to Protestant evangelicalism as a whole. One the one hand, it has contributed to the vitality of religious belief as Christians have read, interpreted, and creatively applied the Scriptures to their own contexts and situations in life. The Word of God gives direction, wisdom, meaning, and hope to millions who meditate individually and corporately on its pages, seeking guidance and comfort from the living God by his living Spirit. The Christian faith today continues to expand around the globe but does not make itself home in a culture until native people can hear the voice of God speaking to them through the Word in their own language. The translation of the Scriptures, as Mark Noll and other international scholars have stressed, is a critical part of the explosive growth of Christianity in Africa and Asia in the latter half of the twentieth century,

---

13. Bornkamm, *Luther in Mid-Career*, 44.

Section 1: The Legacy of Martin Luther and the Reformation

empowering people with a more direct access to God and personal ownership of their faith in their own cultural context.[14]

At the same time, the popular reading of the Bible is what Alistair McGrath has called "Christianity's Dangerous Idea."[15] The Catholic Church was against the translation of the Scriptures and its popular reading, especially after the Reformation began, because it led to a loss of religious uniformity under their control and to potential schism through new competing interpretations. As McGrath states:

> The dangerous new idea, firmly embodied at the heart of the Protestant revolution, was that all Christians have the right to interpret the Bible for themselves. However, it ultimately proved uncontrollable, spawning developments that few at the time could have envisaged or predicted. The great convulsions of the early sixteenth century that historians now call "the Reformation" introduced into the history of Christianity a dangerous new idea that gave rise to an unparalleled degree of creativity and growth, on the one hand, while on the other causing new tensions and debates that, by their very nature, probably lie beyond resolution. The development of Protestantism as a major religious force in the world has been shaped decisively by the creative tensions emerging from this principle.[16]

This indeed was the sad legacy of the Reformation—the division that occurred that ruptured Christian unity, even among Protestants. Agreement on the authority of Scripture, even agreement on theological essentials of salvation, did not equal agreement on other matters such as the sacraments, church government, and predestination. Such religious divisions became wrapped up in early modern statecraft and contributed to the Civil War in England in the 1640s and the Thirty Years War of 1618–48 on the European continent. Religious war even hastened the secularization of Europe as many intellectuals began turning from divisive traditional religion to seek national development and social progress in the authority of more so-called universal foundations in reason and science, while relegating differences of religious belief to individual conscience. Having grown weary of oppression, enforced conformity, persecution, and strife in the name of religion in Europe, modern intellectuals were more ready than ever to theorize and experiment with religious disestablishment, equality, and freedom. The United States was the first of such pioneering governments to encourage complete freedom of religious

---

14. Noll, *Turning Points*, 317–18; Sanneh, *Translating*.
15. McGrath, *Christianity's Dangerous Idea*.
16. Ibid., 2; see also 199–241, 461–70.

competition, which of course included opening the door for the greater influx and toleration of heretical forms of Christianity (Mormonism), other world religions and spiritualities, and even atheism and irreligion as well.[17] Yet McGrath and Noll agree that, despite the denominational divisions and fragmentation of Christianity that inevitably took place as the Scriptures were freed from the dominance of medieval structures of authority, the popular reading of the Bible has contributed to the continued growth, vitality, and dynamic expansion of Christianity as local believers around the world adapt the application of the gospel to transform their cultural contexts.

THE IMPLICATIONS: NEW PERSPECTIVES ON VOCATION, WORK, AND FAMILY LIFE

Luther's theology of justification by faith alone based on the supreme authority of the Scriptures had significant implications for one of the most basic characteristics of human life: work. In the late medieval world, celibate bishops, priests, and monks were held in high esteems as the most godly. Even though marriage was considered a sacrament as it symbolized the mystery of Christ's union with the church, those who had vowed to a celibate life were considered more holy and closer to God than the average married person. Furthermore, the work of bishops, priests, and monks in prayer, teaching, and administration of the sacraments was considered more valuable and pleasing to God than the work of the common farmer, merchant, or homemaking mother.

Luther challenged this mentality as another avenue of works-based righteousness. In his *Address to the Christian Nobility*, Luther addressed the issue of "orders" and "vocation," words that typically were associated with clergy and monastic vows. Luther argued that work does not make one righteous before God, but only faith. Thus, those who have been baptized and have faith in Christ, doing their work to the glory of God and serving the needs of the neighbor, fulfill their special creational calling, whether farmer, baker, or mother. God is pleased thereby, distributing callings to care for the needs of his creation. In fact, Luther could say that God is more pleased by the most ordinary and menial task done by faith, including washing diapers, than a monk who prays a thousand prayers to achieve righteousness before God. Thus, Luther developed the sanctity of all callings in the world on the basis of the common priesthood of the believer. No one vocation is more holy than another as long as it is done with faith and in love for others. All humans,

---

17. Noll, *Turning Points*, 186; McGrath, *Christianity's Dangerous Idea*, 136–49; Gregory, *Unintended Reformation*, 368, 376–81.

Section 1: The Legacy of Martin Luther and the Reformation

including unbelievers, are created to serve as "masks of God" (*larvae Dei*) for others in partnership with him by carrying out their respective callings in the world.

> It follows from this argument that there is no true, basic difference between laymen and priests, princes and bishops, between religious and secular, except for the sake of office and work, but not for the sake of status. They are all of the spiritual estate, all are truly priests, bishops, and popes. But they do not all have the same work to do. . . . Further, everyone must benefit and serve every other by means of his own work or office so that in this way many kinds of work may be done for the bodily and spiritual welfare of the community, just as all the members of the body serve one another [1 Cor 12:14–26].[18]

Of all the "orders" established by God for the care and preservation of the world, Luther held the family (*domus*) in highest esteem as foundational to all the others and "the first order of human life."[19] Luther exhibited the holiness of matrimony and family life by getting married to a runaway nun, Katherine von Bora, in 1525. Against the laws of priestly and monastic vows of celibacy, Luther argued early in a treatise of 1522 that it was perfectly biblical and lawful for a Christian pastor, priest, or other clergy member to forsake such vows and to marry. In fact, it is better to marry than to make false vows of celibacy and be tempted to commit sin.[20] For Luther, it is not necessary to enter a monastery to be tested in faith and obedience to God. Marriage is not only a holy institution created and approved by God but certainly a more-than-adequate environment where faith and love can be tested and exercised against the domination of self-will. Although reluctant to marry given his more dangerous situation and the fact that he was middle-aged, he decided to marry to support his principle of Christian freedom. He and Katherine had several children together, and though it was not a perfect marriage, it was a rather happy marriage, and Luther grew to love and cherish Katherine deeply. After all, Katie effectively managed their whole estate, which was the former Augustinian Cloister in Wittenberg gifted to the Luthers by the prince, and she also administrated their financial holdings that Luther too often wanted to give away. Luther was then able to focus on his pastoral duties, teaching and mentoring of university students, and of course the endless stream of writing. The Luthers often boarded and fed students and other visiting guests in their

---

18. *LW* 44:129–30.
19. Kolb and Arand, *Genius*, 58–64, 112–14; see also Wingren, *Luther on Vocation*.
20. *LW* 45:17–49.

home, enjoying Katie's hospitality as much as their theological table conversations with Luther (although Katie often joined in the conversations, too). Luther once joked that he would soon die if he had to run the estate as busily as she did. The Luther known to history in the years following 1525 would not have been the same without his Katie, who also comforted him through many recurring bouts of depression and health problems.[21]

The sanctity of all callings, especially the family, is an important legacy of Luther's Reformation to Protestant evangelicalism. Although there is still a tendency in Protestantism to uphold pastors and foreign missionaries as doing more spiritual and God-glorifying work than a business manager, farmer, or parent, the Reformation view of vocation is a continual reminder that justification is not by any works whatsoever and that God is pleased when Christians glorify him and serve the needs of others wherever they are called to be and whatever they are called to do. The doctrine of redemption must not throw out the doctrine of creation. God cares for the world he made, and his providence is carried out chiefly through humans, especially as they do their earthly work with faith in Christ and love and justice for others no matter how temporal or mundane the task may seem.

Although it took more than Luther's influence alone to shape the Reformation and the development of an interdenominational Protestant evangelical faith in the centuries that followed, Luther remains a leading source for the development of several key hallmarks associated with modern evangelicalism. These hallmarks are a significant part of what it means to be an evangelical today—to profess total reliance upon Christ by faith for salvation, to nurture a personal relationship with God through reading and meditation on Scripture both individually and in community with others, and to see all earthly callings as important and glorifying to God in serving the needs of others.

Although Luther is more sacramental in his theology and more conservative toward church liturgy than many Baptist and Bible churches would be comfortable with, his theology of justification by faith alone through Christ alone affected a more immediate, direct, and personal access to God in comparison with the barriers established by medieval priestly and papal sacerdotalism. In fact, Lutheran churches in Germany began utilizing more congregational participation in the singing of hymns and moved the altar out from behind the rood screen to be closer to the people. The priest also began facing the people rather than having his back turned to them, reciting the liturgy in German rather than Latin. Although not negating the role of a special calling to pastoral leadership, Luther substantively transformed

---

21. Gritsch, *Wit of Martin Luther*, 99; Trueman, "Life and Death," 184–89; Bornkamm, *Luther in Mid-Career*, 414–15; see also DeRusha, *Katharina & Martin*, 178–91.

Section 1: The Legacy of Martin Luther and the Reformation

the way people thought of the distinction between clergy and laity, increasing the spiritual dignity and privileges of the latter on account of the common priesthood of all sinners and believers in Christ Jesus. This was probably most powerfully demonstrated in Luther's desire that people read and understand the Scriptures for themselves in their own language—a legacy advanced for the English language by William Tyndale who died for the cause in 1536. This did not mean that there was no longer any need for teachers with advanced theological training, but it flowed out of a belief that those things necessary for salvation are plainly spoken by the voice of God in the Scriptures to be read and meditated on by all the faithful for their daily spiritual nourishment and sanctification. It also was a practical rebuke of the current teachers and preachers of religion in Europe who monopolized interpretation of the Scriptures and perpetuated doctrinal error while zealously guarding their claims of privileged status. As McGrath states: "Lay access to the Bible was about power as much as it was about encouraging personal spirituality. The pressure to place the Bible in the hands of the ordinary person was an implicit demand for the emancipation of the laity from clerical domination."[22] Furthermore, the priesthood of all believers meant that priests and monks vowed to celibacy and devoted to prayer, fasting, and preaching were not thereby spiritually superior to shoemakers, merchants, princes, and mothers who serve and work in the home or in the world. For Luther, God has ordered the world and distributed different callings that serve all kinds of human needs, whether in the family or in society at large, which are to be performed faithfully for the benefit of all creation and with thanksgiving to the glory of God.

Thus, the essential spiritual legacy of Luther's Reformation on Protestant evangelicalism was the empowerment of the people with a greater sense of their own spiritual dignity and freedom (although sometimes taking extreme forms that Luther himself did not agree with, as in the case of the Peasants' Revolt). Many of the most dynamic religious movements in Christianity since, and particularly within the history of Protestant evangelical social reform and the missionary movement, have resulted from similar awakenings of ordinary people who become mobilized through personal experience of God and encounters with his Word to take greater initiative, responsibility, and ownership of their faith to impact the world for the glory of Christ.

---

22. McGrath, *Christianity's Dangerous Idea*, 214.

3

Martin Luther's Influence on Politics, the Law, Education, and Economics

Dr. David D. Cook

Martin Luther profoundly impacted the spiritual makeup of the Western world, to be sure. But a look at his life and leadership would be incomplete without at least a brief look at the major contributions he made to the political, educational, legal, and economic structures of the Western world. The Reformation he started sent shock waves throughout Europe, and not just in the spiritual lives of the populous. His frontal assault on the Catholic Church tore down not only the spiritual monopoly of the pope, but forever altered our Western political, economic, legal, and even educational systems.

While the average student of Luther might only focus on his theological contributions, the truth is that he wrote prodigiously on topics ranging from the proper relationship between the church and the state,[1] the prince and his subjects,[2] the role of law in society,[3] the need for universal education,[4] and how a society should care for its poorest members.[5] These writings had a broad-based influence across Europe, from Germany, to Denmark, Sweden,

---

1. *LW* 45:90.
2. *LW* 13:58.
3. *LW* 44:160; *Temporal Authority*, in *LW* 45:90–103.
4. *To the Christian Nobility*, in *LW* 44:205–6; *On Christian Liberty*, in *LW* 44:350–51.
5. *To the Christian Nobility*, in *LW* 44:189–90.

Section 1: The Legacy of Martin Luther and the Reformation

England, and beyond. Unintentionally, his doctrines laid the seeds for future Western movements toward individualism, democracy, and capitalism.[6]

What was it about Luther's movement that allowed it to effect change in all areas of society? Some authors have argued that Reformation theology was the key determinant in societal change.[7] Yet others have argued that theology had little to do with it, but that the pragmatic effects of Luther's writings on education and the law were what made the difference.[8] But I will argue that it was Luther's unique harmonizing of theological concerns with practical considerations that allowed his movement to not just transform the church, but all areas of society. On the one hand, his distinctive blend of doctrines about humanity's relationship to God and humanity's relationship to other Christians in the community laid the cornerstone for a Western Protestant mindset that eventually lent itself toward democracy, capitalism, and a balancing of individual rights and corporate responsibilities. But equally important to this transformation was his and his colleagues' willingness to pragmatically help in the restructuring of society by drafting new legal codes, developing curriculum for public schools, providing guidance on seemingly "secular" matters, and even, in the case of some of his associates, serving in political or judicial posts. Thus, while his theology laid the intellectual foundation for the new structures of Western society, it was his and his colleagues' willingness to proverbially erect scaffolding, lay bricks, and create blueprints that allowed the political, legal, educational, and economic edifices of the Protestant West to emerge.

SETTING THE STAGE: THE POWER OF THE POPE OVER MEDIEVAL SOCIETY PRIOR TO THE REFORMATION

Before Luther emerged on the scene in the early sixteenth century, the Catholic Church dominated all areas of society—not just the "spiritual" realm. Catholic theology recognized the pope as possessing the keys to God's Kingdom on earth. While this meant, first and foremost, that he possessed authority over the body of believers that made up the Church, his power practically extended much further.[9] This was because the Catholic Church saw all of creation as

---

6. Becker et al., "Causes and Consequences"; Bruce, *Did Protestantism Create Democracy*.

7. Weber, *Protestant Ethic*.

8. Becker et al., "Causes and Consequences."

9. "Now, therefore, we declare, say, determine and pronounce that for every human creature it is necessary for salvation to be subject to the authority of the Roman pontiff." Papal Bull ("Unum Sanctum") of Pope Boniface VIII in 1302.

being a part of God's kingdom on earth.[10] Therefore, while the Lord clearly allowed, and even chose, temporal rulers over the people, the pope was God's spiritual agent on earth and held the last word when it came to God's directives for his people.[11] The pope wielded enormous power politically, as he crowned kings, owned an estimated one third of the land in Europe, and even had the power to appoint bishops who held political offices or served as prince-bishops over a particular territory.[12] Because the pope held the power to excommunicate princes and kings, ban the administration of sacraments in territories that challenged him politically, and tax kings and peasants alike in many areas, his political power was enormous by the time of the Reformation.[13] This political power also extended to the legal system. Many of Europe's local territorial laws were in their infancy by the Reformation, whereas the Church's canon law, which had been developed over a thousand years, was extremely comprehensive, touching topics ranging from marriage and divorce, to contract disputes, criminal law, education, and poor laws. In many instances, because of the depth and breadth of this canon law, many litigants, including even the nobility, would choose to have their cases heard in the Church's ecclesiastical courts rather than in their local territorial court system.[14] This stranglehold on the legal system only enhanced the political power of the pope, and made princes and peasants alike subject to his edicts. So, too, did the Church's teachings on poor relief, money-lending, education, and wealth accumulation dominate the economic systems within Europe during this time period. When coupled

---

10. Keller, *Every Good Endeavor*, 68.

11. "We should first be clear about how medieval thinkers understood concepts like church and the temporal realm. In the medieval context of the western world, the notion of Christendom, or a Christian commonwealth, was taken for granted . . . this Christendom was a manifestation of the mystical body of Christ with mystical patterns that composed the details of the mystical body. Within this Christian commonwealth there existed two forces, the *ecclesia* and the *respublica*. Each force was instituted by God and given a role within the mystical body. The *ecclesia*, or church, possessed the power to bind and loose, the *potestas clavium*. The *respublica*, or the temporal power, was the visible agent to whom God had given the power of the sword so that evil might be kept in check. It possessed the *potestas gladii*. The pope was the head of the church. The emperor was the head of the temporal state. In this worldview the state played a negative role. Its task was to hold back the power of evil. However, as we will discover in chapter four, the medieval conception of the *ecclesia* concluded that any power, or sword, possessed by the temporal authorities was essentially on loan from the pope. Thus, all temporal power was controlled, at least conceptually, by the church. With these facts in mind one can conclude that the church was, *de facto*, the primary temporal authority." Montover, "Political and Temporal Dimensions," 22–23.

12. Philpott, "Religious Roots"; Witte, "Law, Religion, and Human Rights."

13. Kurtz, *Church History*, 12.

14. Berman, "Spiritualization of Secular Law," 314–15.

Section 1: The Legacy of Martin Luther and the Reformation

with the heavy tax burdens that bishops imposed in many jurisdictions, these ideals gave the pope power over even the economic spheres of society.[15]

Not only did the pope himself possess great power, but priests, monks, bishops, and other members of the clergy also wielded influence in medieval society. Such sacred members of the clergy were God's chosen representatives on earth, carrying out a *vocatio* ("vocation") that required that they separate themselves from society by remaining celibate and, in the cases of monks, living apart from and removing themselves from society almost completely. By the time of the Reformation, a deeply-rooted theology of spiritual work versus secular work had emerged that devalued the lives and work of lay members of the Church while elevating the power and authority of the clergy.[16] In addition, over hundreds of years, many of the clergy had become quite wealthy and politically powerful. Over time, many wealthy landowners in the West had gifted large tracts of land to the Church or monastic orders, leaving many bishoprics and monasteries with vast landholdings that were producing enormous wealth. Estimates from modern day research show that the Church held as much as one-third of the land in Europe by the time of the Reformation, making it an economic behemoth and a force to be reckoned with on all matters temporal as well as spiritual.

As the Church became ever more prominent, many noblemen sought to make their second and third sons (who could not inherit property or titles under many primogeniture laws) high-ranking officials in the church as an alternative career. This meant that many young men who had no pure desire to become priests, abbots, or bishops became prominent within the church and helped to secularize the functions of the Church. Such intermingling also cemented the political alliances of the pope, as he could then count on the politically powerful fathers and brothers of his clergy to lend aid to his causes. By the time of the Protestant Reformation, these types of ambitious men had made the Church ever more worldly and corrupt, and it became increasingly apparent to even good Catholics that the Church was in great need of reform.

---

15. Ibid.; Ekelund et al., "Economic Analysis"; Montover, "Political and Temporal Dimensions."

16. Whelchel, *How Then Should We Work?*, 62: "In the medieval church, having a vocation or calling referred exclusively to full-time church work.... The ordinary occupations of life—being a peasant farmer or kitchen maid, making tools or clothing, being a soldier or even a king—were acknowledged as necessary but worldly. Such people could be saved, but they were mired in the world."

LUTHER'S THEOLOGICAL FOUNDATION FOR CHANGE IN WESTERN SOCIETY

Into this morass stepped a young monk named Martin Luther who was deeply concerned for the spiritual and physical welfare of the German people. Angered by the corrupt selling of indulgences and what he saw as the oppression of his people, Luther penned his 95 *Theses* and started an ideological revolution. Convicted by the power of the Scriptures and the promise that "the righteous shall live by faith," Luther's doctrines of justification by faith alone and the authority of Scripture alone shook the theological foundations of the Catholic Church in the eyes of many of his followers. With growing forcefulness, Luther attacked not only the authority of the pope and the corrupt practices within the Church, but also the primacy of the ecclesiastical courts, monastic orders, and many of the economic positions held by the Church.[17] As time went on and the Reformation movement grew, Luther's success in tearing down the dominance of the pope, the ecclesiastical courts, Catholic poor laws, and similar institutions left a void in many areas of society. Where once the Catholic Church had provided alms for the poor, educated youth in monastic schools, and decided disputes in ecclesiastical courts, now the Lutheran princes and civic leaders looked to Luther and his fellow Reformers for guidance on how to restructure their society.[18]

Thus, Luther began to step into these raging debates and provided a plethora of practical and theological works that helped to define the Lutheran position on all areas of society.[19] While Luther's doctrines of justification by faith and *sola scriptura* formed the heart of Luther's theological movement, he also developed practical doctrines that helped define the Lutheran position on many seemingly "secular" areas of society. Three of Luther's doctrines, in particular, played important roles in shaping the economic, political, legal, and educational systems within Western society: (1) his doctrine of the priesthood of believers; (2) his conception of the "three estates" in society; and (3) his framing of the "two kingdoms" in the world. While entire books have been written about these doctrines, a brief explanation of each will help outline these topics sufficiently for purposes of the arguments found in this chapter.

---

17. *LW* 44:124–215, 334–73; *LW* 45:245–97.

18. Witte, *Law and Protestantism*, 120: "It was one thing to deconstruct the institutional framework of medieval law, politics, and society with a sharp and skillfully wielded theological sword. It was quite another thing to try to reconstruct a new institutional framework of Evangelical law, politics, and society."

19. *LW* 31, 44, 45.

Section 1: The Legacy of Martin Luther and the Reformation

Luther's Doctrine of the Priesthood of Believers

While Luther's doctrines of justification by faith and *sola scriptura* are seen as the fountainheads of Lutheran theology, Luther's doctrine of the priesthood of all believers may have had an even broader impact on the institutional makeup of society. At the root of prior Catholic theology had been the primacy of the pope and priest over and above the peasant, artisan, or even king. Luther attacked this idea by claiming that all Christians were, by virtue of their baptism, a "royal priesthood":

> How then if they are forced to admit that we are all equally priests, as many of us as are baptized, and by this way we truly are; while to them is committed only the Ministry (ministerium Predigtamf) and consented to by us (nosfro consensu)? If they recognize this they would know that they have no right to exercise power over us (ius imperii, in what has not been committed to them) except insofar as we may have granted it to them, for thus it says in 1 Peter 2, "You are a chosen race, a royal priesthood, a priestly kingdom." In this way we are all priests, as many of us as are Christians. There are indeed priests whom we call ministers. They are chosen from among us, and who do everything in our name. That is a priesthood which is nothing else than the Ministry. Thus 1 Corinthians 4:1: "No one should regard us as anything else than ministers of Christ and dispensers of the mysteries of God."[20]

This idea that all Christian were "priests" had radical consequences. As Montover notes, Luther's "universal priesthood functioned as a fundamental attack on the medieval cosmology which was the root of papal claims of authority in the temporal sphere."[21] Instead of the pope and his prelates having ultimate authority, Luther argued that "every man is responsible for his own faith, and he must see to it for himself that he believes rightly."[22] Faith became individualized, with each Christian going directly to God for confession, salvation, and atonement. This meant that it was important for individual Christians to be able to read the Bible for themselves, understand the sermons preached in church, and have a basic understanding of theology. On a practical level, the Bible needed to be translated into the language of the people, sermons and hymns needed be written in the vernacular, and catechisms needed to be

---

20. *LW* 36:112–13.
21. Montover, "Political and Temporal Dimensions."
22. *LW* 45:108.

drafted which could help the people understand the basics of their responsibilities as Christians.[23]

This shift in theology altered the very core of spiritual authority in Western culture, taking it from the iron grip of the pope and clergy and giving it to the laity. While this doctrine was primarily concerned with spiritual matters, it had ripple effects in many other areas. First, it gave each Christian not only the right, but the responsibility, to start using their individual judgment.[24] While Luther initially argued that this judgment should only be in matters of faith, his writings began to open a door for citizens to start seeing themselves as having the right to possess individual judgment in all areas of society.[25] Likewise, this doctrine created a spirit of egalitarianism among the people, for if every member of the congregation was an equal part of the "royal priesthood" in matters of faith, why should they not also be equal in matters pertaining to secular areas of society?[26] In creating a laity that actively participated in the church, Luther's writings thus also unintentionally created a spirit of activism and participatory engagement in all realms of life. Such activism would eventually sow the seeds for democratic ideals that would shape Western culture.[27]

Luther's Three Estates Theology

While Luther's writings created a spirit of individualism and egalitarianism, he also placed a great emphasis on the duty of each member of society to live together in Christian community. Luther saw society as being comprised of three estates: the family, the church, and the state.[28] As Witte (2002) explains:

> All three of these authorities represented different dimensions of God's presence and authority in the earthly kingdom. All three stood equal before God and before each other in discharging their

---

23. Berman, "Spiritualization of Secular Law," 324.

24. "Besides, if we are all priests, as was said above, and all have one faith, one Gospel, one sacrament, why should we not also have the power to test and judge what is correct or incorrect in matters of faith?" (*LW* 44:135).

25. "From what has been said, every one can pass a safe judgment on all works and laws and make a trustworthy distinction between them, and know who are the blind and ignorant pastors and who are the good and true" (*LW* 31:370).

26. Bruce, "Did Protestantism Create Democracy," 7.

27. "In insisting that everyone could discern the will of God through the reading of his Holy Word, the Reformers shifted the basis of religion from an authoritarian and hierarchical epistemology (in which the truth was available only to a very small number of people) to an essentially democratic one" (ibid.).

28. *LW* 37:364–65.

natural callings. All three were needed to resist the power of sin and the Devil in the earthly kingdom.[29]

Thus, the individual had interconnecting rights and responsibilities with his own family, his local church, and his own government. These duties were grounded in Jesus' command to "love your neighbor as yourself," and undergirded the individual's relationship to all members of society. As Luther noted:

> We will also speak of the things which he does toward his neighbor. A man does not live for himself alone in this mortal body, so as to work for it alone, but he lives also for all men on earth, nay, rather, he lives only for others and not for himself.... Although the Christian is thus free from all works, he ought in this liberty to empty himself, to take upon himself the form of a servant, to be made in the likeness of men, to be found in fashion as a man, and to serve, help and in every way deal with his neighbor as he sees that God through Christ has dealt and still deals with himself.[30]

This strong emphasis on one's responsibilities to the community served as a counterbalance toward egotism and rampant individualism. No man, whether king or beggar, could overstep his bounds since all were part of interconnected estates that had mutual obligations of support and fealty. This community-mindedness did much to cement the bonds of these three estates together, allowing the prince to be seen as the father of his kingdom, the pastor the shepherd of his flock, and each mother and father as being the instructor of their family.

Luther's Two Kingdoms

While Luther saw the interlocking relationships of man as falling under his three estates, he also saw that there were two kingdoms present in the world: the spiritual kingdom and the temporal kingdom. Since Augustine's time, there had been strong emphasis in Catholic theology on the primacy of the "City of City" over the "City of Man."[31] Yet Luther saw these two kingdoms as both having important functions in the life of a Christian.[32] He believed

29. Witte, *Law and Protestantism*, 7.
30. *LW* 37:364–67.
31. Whelchel, *How Then Should We Work?*
32. "God has ordained two kingdoms or realms in which humanity is destined to live, Luther argued: the earthly kingdom and the heavenly kingdom. The earthly kingdom is the realm of creation, of natural and civil life, where a person operates primarily by reason and law. The heavenly kingdom is the realm of redemption, of spiritual and eternal

that the pope should have no more authority over the prince than the prince did over the pope.³³ Each sphere was distinct, yet both worked together to promote Christian community. While the spiritual kingdom concerned itself with matters of faith, which saved men's souls, the temporal kingdom had a very important role in protecting society and promoting virtue:

> For this reason these two kingdoms must be sharply distinguished, and both be permitted to remain; the one to produce piety, the other to bring about external peace and prevent evil deeds; neither is sufficient in the world without the other.³⁴

Just as the three estates in society worked together to promote Christian community in an interconnected web of obligations, so, too, should the two kingdoms be seeking the same goal: the promotion of Christian community. On the one hand, the spiritual kingdom was meant to propagate the faith, deepen Christians understanding of their Lord, and preach against sin. On the other, the temporal state was meant to provide protection, just laws, and stability so that the faithful could love their neighbors properly. The key was that both should have authority over their own duties and should respect the other in its realm of influence as long as both were working toward the same goal of Christian community.³⁵

---

life, where a person operates primarily by faith and love. These two kingdoms embrace parallel heavenly and earthly, spiritual and temporal forms of righteousness and justice, government and order, truth and knowledge. These two kingdoms interact and depend upon each other in a variety of ways, not least through biblical revelation and through the faithful discharge of Christian vocations in the earthly kingdom. But these two kingdoms ultimately remain distinct. . . . A Christian is a citizen of both kingdoms at once and invariably comes under the distinctive government of each" (Witte, *Law and Protestantism*, 5).

33. "It is not proper for the pope to exalt himself above the temporal authorities, save only in spiritual offices such as preaching and absolving. In other things he is to be subject, as Paul and Peter teach, in Romans 13:1, and 1 Peter 2:13, and as I have said above" (*LW* 44:165); "Worldly government has laws which extend no farther than to life and property and what is external upon earth. For over the soul God can and will let no one rule but Himself. Therefore, where temporal power presumes to prescribe laws for the soul, it encroaches upon God's government and only misleads and destroys the souls" (*LW* 45:105).

34. Ibid., 92.

35. Ibid.

Section 1: The Legacy of Martin Luther and the Reformation

THE PRACTICAL STEPS LUTHER TOOK WHICH PROMOTED CHANGE IN WESTERN SOCIETY

The great theological leaps which are described in the sections above no doubt laid a strong intellectual foundation for change within Western society. But what made Luther unique was that he combined this intellectual base with a strong practical push for change. While many other great theologians down the ages have made radical claims which could have shaken their societies, Luther stands apart as a leader who not only challenged the status quo, but helped lay the foundation for a new status quo. His vociferous attacks on the corruption within the Catholic Church coupled with his unique theological arguments convinced many in society that they should reject the old way of doing things. But in turning from Catholic norms, these followers of Luther were left with a void in many areas of their cultural milieu. In response, Luther and his colleagues took an active part in helping to reconstruct society in a way that comported with their comprehensive biblical worldview. From drafting model laws, to writing influential treatises, and preaching about practical cultural issues, Luther stepped into the foray and tried to help the German people and their leaders re-craft society in a way that he felt would be pleasing to God.[36] Along with Luther, colleagues such as Philip Melanchthon, Johannes Bugenhagen, Johannes Brenz, Johannes Eisermann, Johann Oldendorp, and Martin Bucer played important roles in shaping the laws of dozens of cities, provinces, and territories in and around Germany.[37] The practical measures they took to help reform society had broad impacts in many areas. Thus, the next few sections of this chapter will focus on these practical impacts on the political, legal, educational, and economic systems in the West.

Politics

The practical effects of Luther's theology and actions hit at the core of the political framework for much of Western society. As noted above, Luther's attacks on papal authority, when combined with his theological doctrines of priesthood of the believer, the three estates of society, and the two kingdoms of the world, shook the foundations of political thought in Protestant territories. Yet Luther did not stop with these important theological writings. Over his lifetime, he continued to write letters, treatises, and books that covered

---

36. Berman, "Spiritualization of Secular Law," 317.
37. Witte, *Law and Protestantism*, 189–90.

politically important topics such as the role of princes,[38] obedience to rulers,[39] individual rights versus community obligations,[40] and peacemaking.[41] Luther cared deeply about the plight of the German people, and wrote open letters to the nobility to try to entreat them to be "real and good Christians" in the carrying out of their God-given duties as rulers.[42] Likewise, when faced with a violent uprising in Germany by peasants that threatened the peace and stability of the land, Luther wrote vociferously against bloodshed and insurrection.[43] In all, he spent a great deal of time and effort in advocating his political thought to both nobles and commoners alike.

When coupled with his theological doctrines, Luther's advocacy led the way in showing how Christian leaders could influence the political systems of the day. Following the example of Luther, dozens of other Lutheran Reformers likewise stepped into the political arena in order to provide solid leadership focused on biblical principles.[44] In many places, this took the form of serving in political posts, drafting new laws, and helping to reform basic political structures. This political engagement laid a model for Christians to be involved in the temporal affairs of their own governments, and while this involvement was largely centered around Lutheran pastors, theologians, and jurists in the beginning, it also created an ideal which would later be applied to the political involvement of individual laypeople.

While Luther was no proponent of democracy, his own activism coupled with the activism of his colleagues set a tone which would lead later Protestants to advocate strongly for democratic ideals. From a theological standpoint, Luther's doctrines "broke the primacy of corporate Christianity and gave new emphasis to the role of the individual believer."[45] Such individualism also spawned an egalitarianism which had not been present in medieval society.[46] But his writings also invoked a clear call to serve one's neighbor and the

---

38. *To the Christian Nobility*, in *LW* 44:215; *Psalm 82*, in *LW* 13:47–58.
39. *Temporal Authority*, in *LW* 45:111–12; *Psalm 82*, in *LW* 13:42.
40. *On Christian Liberty*, in *LW* 31:344; *Temporal Authority*, in *LW* 45:94.
41. *Psalm 82*, in *LW* 13:42.
42. *Temporal Authority*, in *LW* 45:100.
43. *Keeping Children in School*, in *LW* 46:59–85.
44. Witte, *Law and Protestantism*.
45. Witte, "Law, Religion, and Human Rights," 259.
46. "Protestant doctrines of the person and society were cast into democratic social forms. Since all persons stand equal before God, they must stand equal before God's political agents in the state. Since God has vested all persons with natural liberties of life and belief, the state must assure them of similar civil liberties" (ibid., 260).

Section 1: The Legacy of Martin Luther and the Reformation

community as a whole.[47] When coupled with the idea of individualized faith, this communal shared activism laid the intellectual seeds for later democratic community participation in all areas of society.[48] Likewise, on a pragmatic level, the emerging involvement of so many Protestant laymen in the election of pastors, governance of churches, and propagation of the faith created a model for lay leadership in all areas of society.[49] Likewise, though Luther surely never intended for so many Protestant denominations to spring forth in the coming centuries, the resulting diversity of beliefs gave legitimacy to the ideas that diversity of thought in political matters could likewise be useful and acceptable for society.[50]

In the decades after Luther wrote his 95 *Theses*, the political landscape changed dramatically. Where there had once been a largely homogenous Catholic religious population whose ultimate allegiance lay with the pope, after Luther there emerged a dichotomy between Protestant and Catholic territories. As individuals, prominent merchants, city leaders, nobles, and even princes themselves began to convert to Protestantism, the princes and ruling elites in Protestant territories gained increased power as they shed the authoritarian power of the pope. Suddenly, Protestant princes did not have to pay taxes to the Catholic Church, could confiscate profitable lands owned by the Catholic Church, and became the sole temporal authority in their dominion. Without a strong admonition against tyranny, this could have been a recipe for disaster. But Luther and his colleagues wrote earnestly to the nobles, princes, and common people alike about the proper roles that Christian princes should play in society. Luther argued that rather than being power-hungry despots, Christian princes should be like a father-figure for their kingdoms "seek[ing] the highest good of their subjects."[51] He admonished them that "it is a ter-

---

47. "I set down first these two propositions concerning the liberty and the bondage of the spirit: 1) *A Christian man is a perfectly free lord of all, subject to none.* 2) *A Christian man is a perfectly dutiful servant of all, subject to all*" (*On Christian Liberty*, in LW 1:344).

48. Bruce, "Did Protestantism Create Democracy," 5–10.

49. Ibid.: "To the extent that Protestantism thrived, the old organic feudal community of subservience, descent and fate was displaced by a series of overlapping voluntary democratic associations: the sect's business meeting, the conventicle, the self-organizing prayer group. Protestant sects and denominations themselves formed an important part of the network of civil society but more than that they provided the organizational template for savings banks, workers' educational societies, friendly societies, trade unions and pressure groups. They also provided millions of ordinary people with training in public speaking, in committee management and in small-group leadership. And they provided the persona—the autonomous and self-reliant but caring individual—that could operate the new lay institutions."

50. Ibid., 7.

51. *LW* 44:215.

rible and threatening word against the wicked, self-willed gods, or rulers, for it tells them that they are set over, not wood and stone, not swine and dogs (about which God has made no commandments) but over the 'congregation of God'; and they ought to fear lest the wrong that they do be done against God Himself."[52] Similarly, he admonished princes that it was their duty not to use confiscated Catholic Church lands only for their own profit, but to use those proceeds as a way to help the poor and provide for the common good.[53] In all, the political involvement of Luther and his colleagues created a strong counterbalance against tyrannical rule by princes who were no longer under the authority of the pope.

Over time, and to the great dismay of Luther, wars erupted as Protestant princes fought Catholic princes, peasants fought for freedom in the name of religion, and religious zealots created disharmony in the land. But over the ensuing centuries, the lands which adopted his theological teachings overwhelmingly developed into strong democratic nations.[54] Though he may not have intended it, his doctrines of the priesthood of the believer, the three estates in society, and his writings on the two kingdoms in the world created an intellectual cornerstone for future democratic nations that would balance individual rights with communal obligations. When coupled with his own involvement and the involvement of scores of other Lutheran leaders in helping shape the new political structures of Protestant territories, this combination of thought and action proved to be transformational.

Law

Like their transformational impact on politics, Luther and his colleagues also had a transformational impact on laws and legal systems in the West. The Catholic Church that Luther attacked had dominated the legal sphere of society for centuries, deciding cases on everything from contract law, to property disputes, marriages, crimes, church doctrine, clerical discipline, and civil disputes.[55] Yet Luther's doctrine of the two kingdoms argued that laws should be created by and decided by temporal authorities, leaving the church to deal with truly spiritual matters.[56] On a practical level, he also saw the "intolerable

---

52. *LW* 13:47.
53. Ibid., 53.
54. Bruce, "Did Protestantism Create Democracy"; Witte, "Law, Religion, and Human Rights."
55. Berman, "Spiritualization of Secular Law," 314–15.
56. *To the Christian Nobility*, in *LW* 44:165–66.

Section 1: The Legacy of Martin Luther and the Reformation

injury" that was caused by faraway ecclesiastical judges that "do not know the manners, laws, and customs of the various countries, so that they often do violence to the facts and base their decisions on their own laws and opinions" with "injustice [being] inevitably done the contestants."[57] In place of this far-off system of justice promulgated by a Church that was outside its spiritual authority, Luther advocated for Christian princes who would make laws which would promote godly community. As he noted: "In a word, after the Gospel, or spiritual office, there is on earth no better jewel, no greater treasure, no richer alms, no fairer endowment, no finer possession that a ruler who makes and preserves just laws."[58]

But Luther and his colleagues did not believe that the law should be totally secularized; instead, it should be based on God's natural law and should promote Christian virtue.[59] Not only was the prince the "father" of his kingdom, but he was also the "custodian" of God's natural laws on earth.[60] Philip Melanchthon and others argued that the best codification of natural law was found in the Ten Commandments, which ordered man's relationship to God (commandments 1–3) and man's relationship to his neighbors (commandments 4–10).[61] As "custodian" of the Ten Commandments on earth, the Christian ruler was to be the "voice" of the Ten Commandments within his territory by creating "positive" laws that comported with the values set forth in the Ten Commandments.[62]

57. Ibid., 160.
58. *Psalm 82*, in *LW* 13:54–55.
59. Ibid., 53–55, 90–93.
60. Witte, *Law and Protestantism*, 130.
61. Ibid., 125.
62. Melanchthon had an extensive theory of how the Ten Commandments should play out in the law, and his characterizations formed the basis for modern areas of legal practice: "Melanchthon listed a whole series of positive laws that properly belong under each of the Commandments in the Second Table. On the basis of the Fourth Commandment ('Honor thy father and mother'), magistrates are obligated to prohibit and punish disobedience, disrespect, or disdain of authorities such as parents, political rulers, teachers, employers, masters, and others. On the basis of the Fifth Commandment ('thou shalt not kill'), they are to punish unlawful killing, violence, assault, battery, wrath, hatred, merciliness, and other offenses against one's neighbor. On the basis of the Sixth Commandment ('thou shalt not commit adultery'), they are to prohibit adultery, fornication, unchastity, incontinence, prostitution, pornography, obscenity, and other sexual offenses. On the basis of the Seventh Commandment ('thou shalt not steal'), the are to outlaw theft, burglary, embezzlement, and similar offenses against another's property, as well as waste or noxious use or sumptuous use of one's own property. On the basis of the Eighth Commandment ('thou shalt not bear false witness'), the are to punish all forms of perjury, dishonesty, fraud, defamation, and other violations of a person's reputation or status in the community. Finally, on the basis of the Ninth and Tenth Commandments ('thou shalt

Not coincidentally, the best interpreters of the Ten Commandments were, of course, the Lutheran theologians themselves.[63] This played well into Luther's, Melanchthon's, and their colleagues' plans to play an active part in the restructuring of society. By placing positive law squarely within the confines of natural law, they put themselves in the best position to be able to help godly princes draft and codify laws that properly reflected God's wishes. This they did with vigor; in all, dozens of cities and territories across Germany and Scandinavia began to adopt laws that were either directly written by, or inspired largely upon the writings of Luther, Melanchthon, and other notable Reformers.[64] These Reformers worked together, regularly sending drafts of new laws to their colleagues and asking for comments and suggestions.[65] This collaboration allowed the Reformers to link ideas, create uniformity of laws across vast territories, and inject Reformation theology directly into the very fabric of society.[66] Across Protestant lands, these laws became ingrained in the legal systems and set the tone for jurisprudence for centuries to come.

By taking such an active role in drafting and promulgating new laws, the Lutheran Reformers cemented their theological doctrines firmly into the mainstream of the culture. Thus, while their theological treatises, doctrinal

---

not covet'), they are to punish all attempts to perform these or other offensive acts against another's person, property, reputation, or relationships" (ibid., 133).

63. Ibid.

64. Witte notes: "Luther himself helped to draft the new laws of Leisnig (1523) and Wittenberg (1533 and 1545), and also influenced the reformation ordinances of Gottingen (1530) and Herzberg (1538). Melanchthon's ideas dominated the new reformation laws of Nuremberg (1525), Wittenberg (1533), Herzberg (1538), Cologne (1543), and Meckenburg (1552) and also lay at the heart of the territorial laws of Hesse (1526) and Saxony (1533). Melanchthon also had considerable influence on legal reforms in Tubingen, Frankfurt an der Oder, Leipzig, Rostock, Heidelberg, Marburg, and Jena. Johannes Brenz helped to draft the early reformation laws of Schwabisch-Hall (1526 and 1543) and Brandenburg-Nurnberg (1533) and was the principal draftsman of the massive reformation ordinances of Wurttemberg (1536, 1537, 1553, 1556, 1559). Justus Jonas had a strong influence on the reformation ordinances of Wittenberg (1533, 1545), Saxony (1538), and Halle (1541). Andreas Osiander played a crucial role in negotiating and promulgating the reformation laws of Brandenburg (1533) and Pfalzneuburg (1543). Johann Oldendorp helped to shape the reformation laws of Rostock (1530) . . . Martin Bucer had a strong hand in drafting the new laws of Strasbourg (1524), and Ulm (1531) and also influenced the new reformation laws of Augsburg (1537), Kassel (1539), and Cologne (1543) . . . Bugenhagen drafted the city reformation laws of Brunswick (1528 and 1543), Hamburg (1529), Lubeck (1531), Bremen (1534), and Hildensheim (1544). He also had a strong hand in drafting the laws for the territories of Pomerania (1535), Schleswig-Holstein (1542), Brunswick-Wolfenbuttel (1543), and the Kingdoms of Norway and Denmark (1537)" (ibid., 189–90).

65. Ibid., 15.

66. Ibid., 16; Berman, "Spiritualization of Secular Law," 317.

Section 1: The Legacy of Martin Luther and the Reformation

works, and sermons were incredibly important in shifting the mindset of the German people, the pragmatic steps they took in drafting laws ensured that those ideals were at the forefront of people's everyday lives. As with their work in the political sphere, the Lutheran Reformers' active participation in the restructuring of society, when coupled with their voluminous writing on theological topics, proved to be the catalyst for lasting change in the culture.

Education

While the changes wrought by the Reformers in the political and legal fields were significant, their vision for society could not have been completed without a total reformation of the educational system, as well. By 1500, scholars estimate that less than 1 percent of the German population could read and write.[67] And even among those that were literate, very few could read Latin, rendering them unable to read the Bible in the official Latin Vulgate translation that the Catholic Church had considered sacrosanct for over a thousand years. It is no wonder, then, that the vast majority of people in Germany were at the mercy of the Catholic Church in understanding the Bible and the basics of their own faith. For if people could not read the Scriptures for themselves, they had to rely on priest, bishops, and the pope to tell them what God's Word said for their lives.

Luther saw this as a problem. If man was justified by faith alone, as he believed, then how could a man truly have faith without the ability to read about God for himself? And if every Christian was a part of a royal priesthood who had direct access to God, was it not important for those "priests" to be able to read and discern God's Word for themselves? Finally, if the primary authority for life on earth was the Bible itself, then how could the people understand this authority if they could not read it? The answer to these questions, as Luther saw it, was to educate Christians from all walks of life so that they could read and search the Scriptures for themselves.[68]

Likewise, Luther's doctrine of two kingdoms and his conception of the three estates in society compelled him to advocate strongly for education. In terms of the two kingdoms, Luther saw it as vital to the functioning of the temporal estate that it have a ready supply of educated citizens:

> Now the welfare of a city consists not alone in gathering great treasures and providing solid walls, beautiful buildings, and a goodly supply of guns and armor. Nay, where these abound and reckless

---

67. Becker and Woessmann, "Was Weber Wrong?," 23.
68. *To the Christian Nobility*, in LW 44:205–6.

fools get control of them, the city suffers only the greater loss. But a city's best and highest welfare, safety and strength consist in its having many able, learned, wise, honorable and wellbred citizens; such men can readily gather treasures and all goods, protect them and put them to a good use.[69]

His fellow Reformer Philip Melanchthon echoed this sentiment when he noted that "better letters bring better morals, better morals bring better communities."[70] If the goal of the temporal kingdom was to produce Christian virtue and community, then it would falter mightily unless it had a stock of strong Christian lay leaders trained to take the mantle of leadership for their communities.

As the father of the community, it was incumbent on the prince to educate his citizens, Luther believed.[71] And this education should be for all, not just the elite. Luther advocated strongly for the need to educate nobles and peasants, boys and girls alike.[72] Doing so, he believed, would set up the temporal kingdom for success.[73] Luther suggested that, on a practical level, the funds for such broad-based public education could come from the confiscated lands taken from the Catholic Church[74] and the money that individual taxpayers would have had to pay to the Church.[75]

Luther and his colleagues saw education as not only a way to allow individuals to understand their faith and serve in the community, but also as a way to develop Christian virtue among the populace.[76] In this vein, Luther's three estates doctrine argued that the family, church, and state should all work cooperatively to help shape the Christian virtue of boys and girls.[77] While it was the primary duty of the state to fund and supply public education to all, it was the role of the parents to train their children in Christian love and it was the role of the Church to help them develop a better understanding of God.

69. *LW* 45:355–56.
70. Berman, "Spiritualization of Secular Law," 328–29.
71. Witte, *Law and Protestantism*, 19.
72. *To the Christian Nobility*, in *LW* 44:205–6.
73. "If then there were no soul, as I have said, and if there were no need at all of schools and languages for the sake of the Scriptures and of God, this one consideration should suffice to establish everywhere the very best schools for both boys and girls, namely, that in order outwardly to maintain its temporal estate, the world must have good and skilled men and women, so that the former may rule well over land and people and the latter may keep house and train children and servants aright" (*LW* 45:368).
74. Ibid., 75–76.
75. Ibid., 350–51.
76. Bopart et al., "Protestantism and Education."
77. *To the Christian Nobility*, in *LW* 44:205–6; *On Trade and Usury*, in *LW* 45:245–97.

Section 1: The Legacy of Martin Luther and the Reformation

In promoting this universal education, Luther and his colleagues again took a practical role in helping to reshape society. As a part of almost all of the model laws written by Luther, Melanchthon, and their colleagues, specific statutes relating to public schools and their funding were included for the benefit of all.[78] In addition to these model laws, the Reformers also developed curriculum and advocated for a range of subjects that would help broaden the scope of students' learnings outside of just the study of the Bible itself.[79] Likewise, they advocated for the founding of libraries to house great books that would be available to the community and took pragmatic steps to ensure that the general populace had access to a broad range of important works.[80] Similarly, Luther himself saw such a great need for people to be able to read the Bible for themselves that he devoted almost a year of his life to translating the Bible into the vernacular German language of the people.[81] But it was not enough for people to be able to just read the Bible; Luther wanted them to be able to truly understand their faith. To do this, he wrote a Small and Large Catechism to help train laypeople in the basic doctrines of the faith, and also wrote some of the very first hymns for congregational worship so that, through these songs, people could learn the basics of good theology.[82]

In all, Luther's emphasis on education paid off. In the coming centuries, literacy rates in Protestant territories skyrocketed, and continued to outpace literacy in Catholic territories well into the nineteenth century.[83] This universal education was an important component in creating a climate for democracy in later centuries and, as we shall see in our next section, the rise of capitalism in the West.[84] His emphasis on education not only impacted the theological landscape of Protestant countries, but helped shape the modern literate societies that are present in the West today.

Economics

Finally, Luther's Reformation significantly impacted the economic prosperity of the territories that accepted his ideas. In general, these Protestant lands

78. Berman, "Spiritualization of Secular Law," 328.
79. Ibid., 329; Witte, *Law and Protestantism*, 19.
80. *To the Councilmen of All Cities*, in LW 45:373.
81. Becker and Woessmann, "Was Weber Wrong?," 8.
82. Berman, "Spiritualization of Secular Law," 323–24.
83. Becker et al., "Causes and Consequences," 22.
84. Bruce, *Did Protestantism Create Democracy*, 15; Becker and Woessmann, "Was Weber Wrong?," 3.

have done markedly better in the last five hundred years than their Catholic counterparts, and this phenomenon has been one of the most important social impacts of the Reformation. Many researchers have studied this phenomenon extensively, with a variety of explanations for why the Reformation seemingly caused such a disparity.[85] Max Weber, the great sociologist of the early twentieth century, famously postulated that the economic prowess of Protestant countries was due in large part to the "Protestant work ethic" that was fostered out of Calvinist theology.[86] Under his theory, the Puritans and other hyper-Calvinists who believed in double predestination (the idea that God predestined some to heaven and others to hell) felt the need to work hard and accumulate wealth as a way to provide evidence that they were, in fact, part of God's elect.[87] But many other authors have argued that this explanation is too simplistic to explain such a monumental divide in the economic standings of Protestant and Catholic countries.[88] As they note, not all Protestant countries embraced hyper-Calvinism (many, in fact, were more influenced by Lutheranism than by Calvinism) and the complexities of economic development cannot be whittled down to work ethic alone.

Instead, an emerging line of research has looked at how Luther's focus on education actually had the unintended effect of creating the human capital necessary for modern commerce.[89] Under this theory, it was not work ethic alone that caused economic prosperity, but instead, such prosperity was more likely caused by heightened literacy rates across all social levels of Protestant society. As Bruce (2004) noted, high literacy rates were a "functional prerequisite for economic modernization."[90] In essence, the ability to read and write for oneself laid the economic building blocks for people to move beyond feudalism and toward becoming productive members of a modern society. As Becker and Woessmann noted, such "linguistic and methodical skills created by the teaching of God's Word—reading, understanding, and knowing the Word, including its exegetical comprehension—[were] disposable in relation to other tasks that [went] beyond the religious realm."[91]

---

85. Becker et al., "Causes and Consequences"; Becker and Woessmann, "Was Weber Wrong?"; Bruce, Did Protestantism Create Democracy; Ekelund et al, "Economic Analysis."

86. Weber, *Protestant Ethic*.

87. Becker et al., "Causes and Consequences," 5.

88. Ibid.; Becker and Woessmann, "Was Weber Wrong?"; Bruce, *Did Protestantism Create Democracy*.

89. Ibid.

90. Ibid., 16.

91. Ibid., 9.

Section 1: The Legacy of Martin Luther and the Reformation

Likewise, other authors note that the enormous strides made by Luther and his colleagues in drafting new laws played a part in the economic development of the Protestant West.[92] These new laws, which over time focused more and more on finding a balance between individual rights and community obligations, created a "capitalist communitarianism" that was important for economic development.[93] They also eventually provided new legal innovations such as the joint-stock company and modern trust law which made raising large sums of capital possible. Additionally, new Lutheran social welfare laws created a climate of shared economic growth. While Luther's writings grudgingly allowed for commerce and profit, such economic activities were not to be at the expense of God's command to "love thy neighbor."[94] Thus, this new "capitalist communitarianism" included clear admonitions against usurious practices and for the creation of "community chests" where money could be pooled for the needy in society.[95] The poor laws that Luther and his colleagues wrote in the 1520s, and which soon became the standards across Protestant territories, placed the responsibility on the whole community to care for the needy and promote commerce that would responsibly help all of society. When combined with the budding democratic ideals of later centuries in these Protestant countries, these laws laid a foundation for community cooperation and participation in economic growth.

In all, the most convincing recent research suggests that Luther's work in the fields of politics, the law, and education probably had more to do with Protestant economic success than any other single factor. The human capital that was raised through his focus on literacy, the laws that he and his colleagues drafted, and the seeds they laid for democracy created a cultural milieu that had the pleasant side effect of increased economic prosperity. By transforming society in these other arenas, Luther and his colleagues may have unwittingly created a climate that was ripe for the economic expansion of the 1600s to present in the Protestant West.

---

92. Becker et al., "Causes and Consequences"; Berman, *Law and Revolution*.

93. Ibid.

94. "First,—The merchants have among themselves one common rule, which is their chief maxim and the basis of all their sharp practices. They say: I may sell my goods as dear as I can.... The rule ought to be, not: I may sell my wares as dear as I can or will, but: I may sell my wares as dear as I ought, or as is right and proper. For your selling ought not to be a work that is entirely within your own power and will, without law or limit, as though you were a god and beholden to no one; but because this selling of yours is a work that you perform toward your neighbor, it must be so governed by law and conscience, that you do it without harm and injury to your neighbor, and that you be much more concerned to do him no injury than to make large profits" (*LW* 45:247–48).

95. Ibid., 175.

CONCLUSION

It is no exaggeration to say that Martin Luther had an enormous impact on many areas of Western society. While we may remember him today more for his theology, the truth is that his contributions in the fields of politics, the law, education, and economics also dramatically shaped the world we live in today. It was Luther's unique harmonizing of theological concerns with practical considerations that allowed his movement to not just transform the church, but all areas of society. By being willing to not only write theological treatises, but also actively participate in the restructuring of public institutions, Luther and his colleagues led a Reformation not only of the church, but of all society. The reverberations of these changes can be felt even today, some five hundred years after Luther courageously sparked this transformation.

4

Martin Luther's Impact on Church-State Relations in the West

Dr. Jack Goodyear

If anyone attempted to rule the world by the gospel and to abolish all temporal law and sword on the plea that all are baptized and Christian, and that, according to the gospel, there shall be among them no law or sword—or need for either—pray tell me, friend, what would he be doing? He would be loosing the ropes and chains of the savage wild beasts and letting them bite and mangle everyone, meanwhile insisting that they were harmless, tame, and gentle creatures; but I would have the proof in my wounds.

—Martin Luther[1]

When Martin Luther produced the 95 *Theses* in 1517, he impacted more than just the theological understanding of the Roman Catholic Church and individual salvation. In many respects, Martin Luther's long-lasting legacy influences multiple areas of the culture including the destruction of "the unity of Western Christendom [which] eventually laid the foundation for the

---

1. *Temporal Authority*, in *LW* 45.

modern Western system of religious pluralism."[2] This chapter will examine Luther's view on church and state, while also examining the evolutionary use of Luther's concepts, both positively and negatively, for society.

MARTIN LUTHER'S VIEWS CONCERNING CHURCH AND STATE

The Old Testament prophet Jeremiah, like other prophets in Scripture, received revelation from God and shared it with the people, including rulers and servants. The role of the prophet was not glamorous, and definitely not easy, as many prophets endured mistreatment and ridicule. In Jeremiah 1:19, the LORD commends Jeremiah, saying, "They will fight against you, but they shall not prevail against you, for I am with you, declares the Lord, to deliver you." Luther, like the prophets, is described as one who waited on God's revelation. Longing to hear from the LORD, Luther leaned on the writings of St. Augustine, and depended on the Scriptures to inform him theologically.[3] This personal faith of Luther impacted not only his theological undergirding, but his political and cultural understandings as well.

As the first in his family to receive a formal education, Luther emphasized the importance of education for all individuals, believing that through proper education, people can contribute and serve society effectively.[4] The effective member of society, according to Luther, can only be reformed through the gospel of Jesus Christ. This reformation was not a restoration to a previous exalted state, but rather, simply finding forgiveness by grace through faith in Jesus Christ.[5] However, with Scripture mainly found only in Latin, Luther was convinced that not only Scripture, but all of his writings as well, should be available to the masses, and written in the vernacular German of the people.[6] As people practiced the "priesthood of the believer" in accepting forgiveness from God, the availability of Luther's writings in the language of the people threatened both the powers of the church and the state, which in turn took away from the church both the ability to sell indulgences and "any role in

---

2. Witte, *Religion*, 10.

3. Maddox, "Secular Reformation," 558.

4. Lindberg, *European Reformations*, 372; ibid., 65, also submitted that Luther being the first in his family to receive an education mirrors other Reformers of the era as well, including Melanchthon, Zwingli, and Calvin.

5. Ibid., 10.

6. McGrath, *Reformation Thought*, 89.

Section 1: The Legacy of Martin Luther and the Reformation

forgiveness, thereby threatening the vested interests of the pope, many clergy, some princes, and one rather important banking house."[7]

Luther's break from the church in his theological emphasis on the priesthood of the believer further escalated his opposition to the pope. In Luther's *Address to the German Nobility*, Luther writes: "Whoever comes out of the water of baptism can boast that his is already consecrated priest, bishop, and pope."[8] With church and state so entwined during Luther's time, an assumed criticism against the church included a threat to the public order as well, which in turn led many rulers to forbid those living in their territories from having access to or from reading any of Luther's writings, including his translation of the Scripture.[9] Luther voiced his opposition to the rulers, writing, "Thus they neatly put the shoe on the wrong foot: they rule the souls with iron and the bodies with letters, so that worldly princes rule in a spiritual way, and spiritual princes rule in a worldly way."[10] This statement reveals Luther's concept of two kingdoms, which contains his views on the responsibilities of government and the church, and which includes the proper use of coercion and persuasion.

Luther's lasting contribution to church-state studies includes his dichotomy between coercion and persuasion. One kingdom, the temporal kingdom, oversees the body and the physical society, using coercion when necessary to control humanity. The other kingdom, the spiritual kingdom, uses persuasion to impact the soul of the believer. For Luther, the spiritual kingdom should avoid coercion, since the Holy Spirit will move in the lives of believers. Coercion is left to the state. In other words, the believer responds to God's grace; the public responds to state actions.[11]

Considering proper authority, the spiritual kingdom is overseen by the church, and includes the Word of God and the sacraments of the church. The temporal kingdom encompasses the secular government, or state, and

---

7. Ibid., 117. With Luther's theological teaching, people no longer needed to make payments to cover their "sins." Forgiveness was a private affair, not public, so the individual was free from the need for government to orchestrate forgiveness, or the priest to authorize forgiveness.

8. Luther, quoted in Gritsch, "Martin Luther and Violence," 41.

9. Sockness, "Luther's Two Kingdoms," 94. See also Gritsch, "Martin Luther and Violence," 42, where some rulers viewed Luther as a potential liberator, which threatened order.

10. Luther, quoted in Sockness, "Luther's Two Kingdoms," 98.

11. McGrath, *Reformation Thought*, 225. See also Sockness, "Luther's Two Kingdoms," 96, where he quotes Luther from *Temporal Authority* as writing, "We must divide the children of Adam and all mankind into two classes, the first belonging to the kingdom of God, the second to the kingdom of the world."

includes emperors, rulers, and citizens.[12] When it comes to dealing with the evils of the world, the spiritual kingdom is to endure the evil by waiting on God and by practicing forgiveness; however, the temporal kingdom utilizes the sword to contain wickedness and restrain actions detrimental to society.[13] The two kingdoms are distinct, and the temporal kingdom should not interfere with the spiritual; however, the spiritual still dwells under the realm of the temporal.[14] Through this passage, Luther viewed the state, while overseeing the worldly, or secular, realm, as still performing a divine role.[15] But Luther limits the role of the state in any attempt to coerce on behalf of the spiritual realm, arguing that the temporal kingdom should never use force to promote or protect the gospel.[16] Faith is personal, free from coercion. Order is necessary, and enforced through governmental coercion. For Luther, both kingdoms needed each other for existence and survival: "For this reason God has ordained two governments: the spiritual, by which the Holy Spirit produces Christians and righteous people under Christ; and the temporal, which restrains the un-Christian and wicked so that—no thanks to them—they are obliged to keep still and maintain an outward peace."[17] While Luther separated the two spheres into the temporal and spiritual, it is clear that according to Luther, this division actually allowed for the harmonizing of conflicts between the two spheres by keeping their responsibilities distinct.[18]

To better understand Luther's view of the temporal kingdom, one should examine Luther's view of humanity and the state. Breaking from the tradition that viewed humanity as just and good, Luther taught that the individual is corrupt and sinful.[19] Luther's writings are described as "laced with deep pessimism about the capacity of social actors to engage in unselfish action."[20] With this understanding, Luther believed only the gospel could restore the individual; however, the state would need to contain the chaos by coercively controlling through the civil law the actions of others. Luther advocated that "stern, hard civil rule is necessary in the world, lest the world become wild,

---

12. Whitford, "Cura Religionis," 44.
13. Herman, "Luther, Law, and Social Covenants," 96.
14. Sockness, "Luther's Two Kingdoms," 94. Sockness describes Luther's *Temporal Authority*, as his "most careful, systematic, cool-headed attempt to explicate the nature of responsible Christian existence in a sinful world."
15. McGrath, *Reformation Thought*, 224.
16. Lindberg, *European Reformations*, 367.
17. Luther, quoted in Sockness, "Luther's Two Kingdoms," 96.
18. Ibid., 95.
19. Berman, "Religious Foundations," 17.
20. Herman, "Luther, Law, and Social Covenants," 260.

Section 1: The Legacy of Martin Luther and the Reformation

peace vanish, and commerce and common interest be destroyed.... The civil sword shall be red and bloody" through the rule of law.[21] According to Luther, the proper role for civil government included keeping the society from devolving into chaos, while specifically limiting unlawful or harmful actions.[22]

Although Luther viewed the civil government as possessing the power to squash incivility, he also wished to confine governments to the secular realm. However, Luther expected secular authority to promote laws and practices that would benefit the well-being of the citizens.[23] For Luther, this protection included the weak and powerless, and this imperative being based on the divine call from Psalm 82 to "give justice to the weak and the fatherless; maintain the right of the afflicted and the destitute"[24] Additionally, Luther needed the political authority on his side in order to receive the civil backing he needed for the Reformation. By giving the state a role in overseeing the temporal realm, Luther effectively brought in the state to help control any repercussions he might receive from the church.[25]

Emphasizing the common good, Luther's charge to secular authority to seek the common good differs from his contemporary, Niccolo Machiavelli. Whereas Luther conveys the view that the prince of a region should serve his people, even in the secular state, Machiavelli endorsed the raw use of power, caring little for the needs of the people. Luther's inclusion of a moral compass for secular authority is an important component in understanding his separation of the two kingdoms.[26] However, even so, Luther expected the citizens to obey authority, regardless of whether the secular state acted justly or not.[27] Even wicked actions, according to Luther, would not justify rebellion, as he stated: "The fact that the rulers are wicked and unjust does not excuse disorder and rebellion."[28] As will be noted later, this philosophy led to dire complica-

---

21. Luther, quoted in Berman, "Religious Foundations," 19.

22. Soper, "Differing Perspectives," 17. See also Whitford, "Cura Religionis," 48, where he quotes Luther: "If God grants man power over life and death, surely He also grants power over what is less, such as property, the home, wife, children, servants, and fields. All these God wants to be subject to the power of certain human beings, in order that they may punish the guilty."

23. Herman, "Luther, Law, and Social Covenants," 262.

24. Whitford, "Cura Religionis," 55.

25. McGrath, *Reformation Thought*, 227.

26. Berman, "Religious Foundations," 16.

27. Herman, "Luther, Law, and Social Covenants," 263. See also Sockness, "Luther's Two Kingdoms," where he quotes Luther as writing, "Christians are obligated to serve the state as they perform all other works of love—not out of their own need, but solely out of the need of their neighbors."

28. Luther, quoted in McGrath, *Reformation Thought*, 226.

tions at times throughout history, as people seeking to live out Luther's teachings struggled with how to respond to governments that performed evil acts.

In an attempt to limit the temporal kingdom, Luther confined the state from entering into theological decisions of the church. Luther viewed the state role as only dealing with the outward actions of the citizen, not with the spiritual decisions of conscience, which was the proper domain of the church, or spiritual kingdom: "Where the temporal authority presumes to prescribe laws for the soul, it encroaches upon God's government and only misleads souls and destroys them."[29] As long as the secular authorities allowed Christians to exercise their faith, Luther taught that it was the rightful duty of the citizens to obey authority and accept the status quo of the temporal realm.[30] For Luther, the dutiful citizen obeys the law, performs good works as a service to others, avoids evil, and realizes that salvation does not come from these actions, but only through the grace of God.[31]

Luther was content with teaching Christians to obey the temporal authorities due to his belief that Christians who lived proper lives guided by the Holy Spirit would fear little from the government.[32] However, this obedience was dependent upon the temporal realm remaining outside of the spiritual realm's oversight of human salvation. The temporal realm, according to Luther, should play no role in coercing individuals to accept salvation through God. While the temporal authority can coerce the obedience of physical actions of the individual, it plays no part on personal salvation, as Luther writes, "For faith is a free act, to which no one can be forced. Indeed, it is a work of God in the spirit, not something which outward authority should compel or create."[33] With government relegated to the temporal realm, Christians were responsible in the spiritual realm for relying on the Word of God, not politics, for salvation. Luther taught that the spiritual kingdom was eternal and encompassed the gospel, revelation from God, and personal faith. Embedded in his understanding included freedom and equality for the individual before God, and the responsibility of the individual to determine the path for his or her beliefs.[34] The individual decision to follow God was outside the enforcement of

---

29. Luther, quoted in Sockness, "Luther's Two Kingdoms," 97.
30. Soper, "Differing Perspectives" 17.
31. Berman, "Religious Foundations," 17.
32. Sockness, "Luther's Two Kingdoms," 96. Luther is quoted as writing, "True Christians need no law because, being righteous, they freely (like good trees bearing good fruit) do more than the law demands."
33. Luther, quoted in ibid., 97.
34. Whitford, "Cura Religionis," 44.

Section 1: The Legacy of Martin Luther and the Reformation

any entity, for, as Luther stated, "What is free cannot be compelled."[35] Instead, those in the spiritual realm must rely on the Spirit for guidance.

This freedom also protected the individual from the spiritual authority. Having wrestled personally with his theological beliefs, Luther desired to limit papal authority in the spiritual realm, withdrawing from the church in general, and the pope specifically, the ability to legally enforce theological edicts. Luther also intended for this limitation of papal authority to include limiting the ability of the pope to change theology and scriptural interpretations.[36] Instead, Luther advocated for the church to be "purely a spiritual community, part of the heavenly realm of peace, joy, grace, salvation, and glory."[37] To limit papal authority, under his philosophy of the two kingdoms, Luther maintained that the church, being found in the world, must submit to the temporal authority in matters beyond the spiritual realm, while also recognizing the spiritual worth of each individual regardless of position.[38] Again, Luther did not believe the church should interfere with the responsibilities of the state, regardless of the actions of the state.[39]

For Luther, a pragmatic political authority would enact justice in the temporal realm, while the church would allow the Holy Spirit to guide believers in the spiritual realm. Luther's approach is influenced by his belief that the two realms often erroneously confused roles, which in turn signified the need for a reformation.[40] If the church governed by force, Luther concluded that the power of God's grace would be lost. Likewise, if the state turned the other cheek, then chaos would reign in society.[41] However, the situation for some grew more complicated when the secular authority enacted practices that caused oppression or injustice. For Christians in the spiritual realm who wished to intercede, Luther warned against such crossover between realms, instead assuring that God's purposes would be worked out through the Spirit:

---

35. Lindberg, *European Reformations*, 107.

36. Wolin, "Politics and Religion," 27.

37. Berman, "Religious Foundations," 15. See also McGrath, *Reformation Thought*, 88.

38. McGrath, *Reformation Thought*, 222. Luther wrote, "It is pure invention that pope, bishop, priests, and monks are called the spiritual estate, while princes, lords, artisans, and farmers are called the temporal estate. . . . All Christians are truly of the spiritual estate, and there is no difference between them except that of office."

39. Ibid., 225. McGrath discusses how Luther faulted the peasants during the Peasant Revolt for attempting to revolt against the temporal authority of the state.

40. Mitchell, "Protestant Thought," 691. See also Berman, "Religious Foundations," 14, where he writes, "The Lutheran reformation and the revolution of the German principalities that embodies it, broke the Roman Catholic dualism of ecclesiastical and secular law by delegalizing the church."

41. Whitford, "Cura Religionis," 52.

"There is no need for you to demand an armed insurrection. Christ himself has already begun an insurrection with his mouth, one which will be more than any pope or any man can bear."[42] Luther also encouraged those experiencing injustice from the temporal realm, conveying to them that any amount of hardship they are enduring will strengthen their individual character and spiritual development.[43] The temporal realm had the authority from God to inflict violence in protection of the state, while the individual in the spiritual realm must be willing to suffer political violence rather than resist it.[44]

To justify his philosophical approach to the two kingdoms, Luther leaned on the Sermon on the Mount as most authoritative for those in the spiritual realm, while citing Romans 13 as granting the necessary authority to the temporal realm. Romans 13:1–7 is a pivotal text in how one views governmental authority. In the passage, the author writes, "Let every person be subject to the governing authorities. For there is no authority except from God has established, and those that exist have been instituted by God." The way one interprets the passage dictates how one responds to an oppressive government. For Luther, he interpreted Romans 13 as specifically forbidding Christians from resisting the temporal realm: "It is better for the tyrants to wrong them a hundred times than for the mob to treat the tyrant unjustly but once."[45] Luther believed that God forbade insurrection, since the practice of insurrection would tend to remove God's glory from the center of life and replace it with humanity's understanding of what should or should not be.[46]

From Luther's theology, one can deduce major premises concerning Christians and politics. Christian ethics is informed by faith alone, which compels the Christian to engage in proper civic responsibilities. These civic responsibilities must conform to the will of the secular authority, as determined by God. Because the state is appointed by God, under the interpretation of Luther, the church should not attempt to have any authority over the state, instead, the church should abide by the gospel and the Sermon on the Mount, allowing the Spirit to move in lives within the spiritual realm, while practicing obedience to the state in the temporal realm.[47] With Romans 13 as guidance, citizens should dutifully abide by the direction and leadership of the temporal authority, recognizing that the authority was placed there by God, according to Luther's interpretation.

42. Luther, quoted in Gritsch, "Martin Luther and Violence," 44.
43. Herman, "Luther, Law, and Social Covenants," 263.
44. Gritsch, "Martin Luther and Violence," 52.
45. Sockness, "Luther's Two Kingdoms," 106.
46. Gritsch, "Martin Luther and Violence," 44.
47. Ibid.

Section 1: The Legacy of Martin Luther and the Reformation

Over time, Luther's propensity toward obedience to the temporal authority without question led to a shift in his structural understanding of balancing church and state interaction within sovereign territories. He began to shift away from a pure two-kingdom approach to a *cura religionis* approach, which placed the temporal authority of an area as having the charge to be "the custodian of both tables of the law, to regulate the right order of true religion."[48] This shift placed more authority and responsibility into the hands of the magistrate, requiring more of a submission of the spiritual kingdom to the temporal one. As a result of the Reformation, societies dealt with a growth of religious pluralism, which potentially caused conflicts for regions not only concerning religion, but also concerning social structures and cultural viewpoints as well.[49] Continuing his evolution, Luther embraced an additional shift in church-state relations: *cuius region, eius religio*.[50] This nuanced approach attempted to solve tensions and conflicts created by multiple religions existing in a single territory.[51]

Luther's eventual shift to *cuius region, eius religio*, inspired changes among various countries' laws, including Germany. As a result of the influence of Lutheran thought, the changes included: (1) The prince became the head of the church; (2) A secular civil service was created to advise the prince; and (3) A secularization of laws dealing with marriage, divorce, crimes, property, and other contracts, which came under the influence of the state.[52] While Luther's viewpoint took a step toward full religious liberty by divorcing the enforcement of faith by the church, it was still a far cry from complete religious liberty. Further, it should be noted that Luther was not the only Reformer on the scene. As Luther developed his understanding of the society in light of the Reformation, other Reformers, including Ulrich Zwingli and John Calvin, were adapting Lutheran thought to their contexts. While Luther may have preferred a monarchical structure of government to maintain his viewpoints, Zwingli distrusted the monarch, believing eventually all monarchs become tyrants, and instead embraced a more democratic form of government. Calvin, rejecting the submission of the church to the temporal realm, placed the church back at the center of governmental life.[53] These two thinkers, in addi-

---

48. Whitford, "Cura Religionis," 42.

49. Lindberg, *European Reformations*, 359.

50. "Whose realm, his religion." This viewpoint attempted to solve the pluralism issue by authorizing the faith of the ruler as the predominant faith for the territory.

51. Harrington and Smith, "Confessionalization," 77.

52. Berman, "Religious Foundations," 18.

53. McGrath, *Reformation Thought*, 227. See also Berman, "Religious Foundations," 26.

tion to Luther, continue to influence the aftermath of the Reformation, not just theologically, but societally as well. The Reformation impacted all areas of society. Luther's understanding of church and state interaction, continues to drive responses in the West to the realities of religious pluralism and political power.

Luther's Advocacy for Conscience: Toward American Freedom

From his famous Diet of Worms Speech in 1521, Luther said, "My conscience is captive to the Word of God. I cannot and will not retract anything, for it is neither safe nor right to go against conscience. I cannot do otherwise, here I stand, may God help me."[54] With Luther's claim to his conscience, one can deduce the development of the doctrinal position Luther held that could lead to the rise of democratic thought.[55] However, one should not confuse Luther for the champion of democratic freedom. After all, he did authorize the death of dissenters, such as Anabaptists, for example; however, as one historian notes, "The Protestant Reformation itself has at times been credited with the rise of religious liberty," even if such a statement must be made "only with distinct reserve."[56] Luther's reforms, and his emphasis on the conscience of the believer, is credited partially as the originator of individualism in political thought, which leads historians to conclude that the Reformation tends to bend toward democracy.[57] One can trace the influence of Luther's thought to the development of freedom in the New World. For the focus of this chapter, Luther's influence on John Locke and Roger Williams will be paramount.

One of the major influencers of American political thought was John Locke, seventeenth-century English philosopher. In Locke's *Letter Concerning Toleration* (1689), Locke distinguishes between state authority and religious authority, echoing a similar strain of thought within Luther's two-kingdom model.[58] Like Luther, Locke argued that the two spheres needed separation due to the confusion of roles: the religious authority was too involved in

---

54. Luther, quoted in Lindberg, *European Reformations*, 361.
55. Ibid., 362.
56. Bainton, "Struggle for Religious Liberty," 95.
57. Maddox, "Secular Reformation," 559. See also Lindberg, *European Reformations*, 361–62, where he wrote, "Protestant arguments for resistance to tyranny continued to ferment political change in the eighteenth-century American and French revolutions."
58. Roover and Balagangadhara, "John Locke," 532. The authors state, "[Locke's] basic conceptual scheme is virtually identical to that of the theology of Christian liberty."

Section 1: The Legacy of Martin Luther and the Reformation

secular responsibilities and the secular authority too involved in religious issues.[59] Concerning coercion and the church, Locke wrote:

> If anyone maintain that men ought to be compelled by fire and sword to profess certain doctrines, and conform to this or that exterior worship, without any regard had unto their morals; if anyone endeavour to convert those that are erroneous unto the faith, by forcing them to profess things that they do not believe and allowing them to practise things that the Gospel does not permit, it cannot be doubted indeed but such a one is desirous to have a numerous assembly joined in the same profession with himself; but that he principally intends by those means to compose a truly Christian Church is altogether incredible. It is not, therefore, to be wondered at if those who do not really contend for the advancement of the true religion, and of the Church of Christ, make use of arms that do not belong to the Christian warfare.[60]

Locke advocates for the separation of responsibilities of the church and the state, advocating for the spiritual realm to reject coercion as a power to compel belief. Like Luther, civil interests and religious issues should be separated. Seen as a "secularized replica of the theological model" established by Luther, Locke's influence on American development of religious liberty contains ties to the Lutheran Reformation.[61]

Likewise, Roger Williams profoundly influenced the American understanding of church and state relations as well. Williams' push for religious liberty in the New World, first in Massachusetts and then in Rhode Island, coupled with his teachings, advocated for the liberty of the conscience and ability to practice faith or no faith for each individual, without fear of reprisal from either the church or the state. According to one historian, Williams "pushed to extremes the principle of Luther that the State is not to be regarded as a Christian institution."[62] When historians focus on the development of religious liberty in the United States, much credence is given to two groups: Enlightenment thinkers and Evangelical Protestants, like Baptists. John Locke and Roger Williams represent key figures in each of those categories, thus connecting the work of Luther to the development of religious liberty in the United States. For example, Thomas Jefferson, who was heavily influenced by John Locke's writings and championed by evangelicals who desired religious freedom and separation of church and state, routinely referenced the

59. Mitchell, "Protestant Thought," 691.
60. Locke, *Letter Concerning Toleration*, 5.
61. De Roover and Balagangadhara, "John Locke," 526, 532.
62. Bainton, "Struggle for Religious Liberty," 224.

importance of conscience, like Luther, in his arguments for separation of the temporal and spiritual realms.[63] The influence of the two kingdoms argued for by Luther continues to be felt in the United States.

Luther's Advocacy for Order: Toward German Oppression

While American thought on the proper role of the church and the state more closely resembled Luther's depiction of the two kingdoms, Germany's approach followed Luther's nuanced understanding of *cuius region, eius religio*. The implications from the path Germany followed led the government to a different understanding of the role of the church and the state compared to America. Luther is criticized for giving too much sway to the secular state, with little allowance for religious dissent.[64] While Luther expected secular authority to pursue the common good of the citizens, his insistence that Christians not retaliate against injustice complicated the church's response during times of true oppression from the state. A clear example of this complication is found in Hitler's Germany.

During the rise of the Third Reich, the prevailing political mood among the German people, particularly the conservatives, "yearned for authority, hierarchy, true allegiance, salvation from communism, and for a strong central state and strong traditional values in the world of urban industrialization and pluralism."[65] Alarmed at the perceived changing values in Germany brought on by pluralism, German leaders began to appropriate the teachings of Luther as justification for the people to place trust in the government to use "religion" to strengthen the moral fiber of the nation. This rise of nationalism, coupled with the theological framework which compelled Christians to set aside their ethical questions when it came to obeying governmental authority, created an atmosphere ripe for the expansion of Nazism.

One prominent theologian in Germany during this time was Emanuel Hirsch, who also claimed membership in the Nazi party. Hirsch's educational and religious foundation was influenced by Karl Holl, a German scholar who created a "Luther-Renaissance" in Germany prior to World War II.[66] Viewing Hitler as an authority that could reclaim German significance, Hirsch played an instrumental, theological role in advocating for the German people to place complete trust in Hitler as leader, arguing, "God is affirmed to be behind

---

63. De Rooveer and Balangangadhara, "John Locke," 537.
64. Whitford, "Cura Religionis," 45.
65. Stroup, "Political Theology," 322.
66. Ibid., 341.

Section 1: The Legacy of Martin Luther and the Reformation

all of history and to meet us in its events, in that we are constantly called upon to shape events by decisions."[67] By grounding his interpretation of Lutheran theology in Romans 13, Hirsch warned of the dire consequences facing Germany if the Christian church "failed to show awareness of God's hand in the religious revival accompanying the National Socialist revolution," also known as the Nazi Party.[68] Going further, Hirsch even warned that "only those sympathetic to Hitler be fully supported as church leaders."[69] This use of Lutheran interpretation of church and state proved to be detrimentally influential to the Christian church in Germany, making it difficult for the Christian opposition to Hitler and Nazism to be given audience.

Hirsch's success in using Lutheran theology to approve of the Nazi Party was not fully supported by all leaders in the church, however. Karl Barth, a contemporary of Hirsch, savaged this interpretation of theology, labeling Hirsch's view of Luther as the justification for the "fountain of German Hitlerism."[70] Additionally, Dietrich Bonhoeffer resisted the temptation to ignore the atrocities of the Nazi party and struggled with his church's theology concerning state authority. Ultimately, he opposed Hitler and Nazism, which eventually cost him his life. Through his speeches and writings, Bonhoeffer called upon the church in Germany to question the injustices of the Nazi regime and protect those oppressed and persecuted by it. Further, not only did Bonhoeffer reject the notion that Hitler was part of God's divine plan, he called upon Christians to "fall into the spokes of the wheel itself," and attempt to stop the atrocities.[71] Bonhoeffer went on to proclaim, "I pray for the defeat of my country, for I think that is the only possibility of paying for all the suffering that my country has caused the world."[72]

While Bonhoeffer ultimately lost his life, the church in Germany, influenced by a theology that rejected the church's right to resist the state, allowed for the domination of the state over the church. As one historian noted, "The failure of the German church to oppose Hitler in the 1930s is widely seen as reflecting the inadequacies of Luther's political thought. Even Hitler, it appeared to some German Christians, was an instrument of God."[73] Reinhold Niebuhr,

---

67. Ibid., 347.
68. Ibid., 349.
69. Ibid., 352.
70. Gritsch, "Martin Luther and Violence," 38.
71. Rankin, "Dietrich Bonhoeffer," 113.
72. Bonhoeffer, quoted in ibid., 115. Bonhoeffer also said, "If we claim to be Christians, there is no room for expediency. Hitler is anti-Christ. Therefore, we must go on with our work and eliminate him whether he is successful or not."
73. McGrath, *Reformation Thought*, 226.

a prominent American theologian during the twentieth century, extended his criticism to Luther's concept of the two kingdoms and the ultimate use of the theory in Nazi Germany, decrying the submission of the church to the power of the state for the sake of order:

> It gave government and principle of order an absolute preference over rebellion and political chaos. This one exception had morally catastrophic consequences. It tended to ally the Christian church too uncritically with the centres of power in political life and tempted it to forget that government is frequently the primary source of injustice and oppression.[74]

The desire for security and order routinely conflicts with individual freedom and conscience. Whereas the founding of the United States embraced the conscience, 1930s Germany opted for societal order. The inadequate response of the German church to Hitler's actions reveals the limitations on Luther's conclusions regarding the two kingdoms. After all, faith without action is dead.[75]

CONCLUSION

Any attempt to understand the repercussions of one's theological and political teachings is not without limitations. Luther's teachings concerning church and state were specific to his context, one of political and theological dominion. However, the evolution of Luther's depiction of the two kingdoms to the United States and Germany, for example, demonstrates the complexity and unpredictability of developing philosophies. While Luther neither advocated for a democracy like the United States nor for an evil state like Nazism, his teachings through time were used in both instances to justify certain actions. As a student of history, one must learn from motivations that lead to various uses or abuses of concepts or theories. As one historian wrote:

> Having seen the motivation and results of Hirsch's abandonment of the separation of religion and politics, can contemporary non-Nazi political theologians avoid comparable disasters? Or will future historians be forced to conclude that any mixing of theology with politics must lead to enthusiastic fanaticism, zealotry, and the sanctification of ideological holy war?[76]

---

74. Niebuhr, *Nature and Destiny*, 221.
75. Gritsch, "Martin Luther and Violence," 55.
76. Stroup, "Political Theology," 353.

Section 1: The Legacy of Martin Luther and the Reformation

Luther, Locke, Williams, Bonhoeffer and others wrestled with the balance of the realms comprised of the church and the state. In many ways, this is a uniquely Christian problem. This problem, while at times creating inconvenience, is actually a healthy problem for a society to have: "That there is tension, even conflict, between church and state is not only inevitable, but ought to be welcomed, for the Christian ought to understand that the conflict can never be completely resolved."[77] With that, the modern understanding of religious liberty is indebted to Luther's boldness in beginning the Reformation. However, the challenge facing society today is how to maintain the tension between the two realms while also protecting the dignity of each individual.

---

77. Wood, "Christianity," 270.

SECTION 2

Assessing Martin Luther's Leadership

5

Martin Luther's Leadership as a Change Agent

Dr. David D. Cook

The legacy of any leader can be measured by the positive change he cements in his own organization, nation, or culture. While many leaders across the millennia have created change in their society, few have caused such broad-based change as Martin Luther. Someone surveying Europe in 1600 would have found a cultural milieu that was markedly different than what was present just a hundred years before, in 1500. For a society that had not changed markedly in a thousand years, the seismic shift that Luther brought in the span of a few decades was remarkable. From the church, to government, law, education, and economics, the hue of society was drastically different because of the leadership of Martin Luther and his fellow Reformers.

So what was it that made Martin Luther such an effective change agent? Many other potential Reformers before him, such as John Hus, John Wycliffe, and Girolamo Savonarola, had largely failed in their attempts to end corruption and despotism within the Catholic Church. Yet in the face of many of the same challenges they faced, Luther prevailed. Not only did he prevail, but he did so on a broad scale. Nations that had once been wholly Catholic became Protestant; canon laws that had overshadowed local laws were replaced with new legal codes; education that had once been monopolized by the Church was opened to all of society; and people who had once had to go to a priest to get to God felt that they could now have a real relationship with their Creator.

Section 2: Assessing Martin Luther's Leadership

These were but a few of the remarkable changes put into motion by the Protestant Reformation that Luther sparked.

This chapter will examine Martin Luther's leadership as a change agent. In applying John Kotter's (1996) change model, I will argue that, unlike his predecessors, Luther succeeded in creating broad changes in society because he established a sense of urgency, built a guiding coalition, communicated extremely well, removed structural obstacles to change, engaged in activities that would cement change into the minds and hearts of the people who followed him, and carried out a change initiative that closely aligned with all eight steps of Kotter's seminal model of change. In applying this modern theory of change to Martin Luther, I hope to show contemporary leaders of today how they can apply similar lessons to their own cultural contexts.

SETTING THE STAGE

Even in Martin Luther's day, the world was changing, albeit at a much slower pace before he arrived. The Catholic Church had largely dominated the Western world for a thousand years, and was cemented as the spiritual, political, economic, and educational status quo in society. Yet in the century before Luther, the printing press invented by Johannes Gutenberg in 1440 had dramatically altered the flow of ideas in Europe.[1] For the first time, great thinkers could disseminate their works rapidly across a broad expanse of society, opening the way for revolutionary ideas (such as Luther's) to spark great movements. Likewise, exploration around the world by intrepid explorers in the 1400s and early 1500s opened up a world of possibilities as Europeans realized that they could interact with a broader group of people half a world away and that the world was not as tiny as they had once imagined.

Yet despite the magnitude of these changes, life for most Europeans was largely the same as it had been a thousand years before. Peasants were bound to their lords in an unending cycle of poverty and powerlessness; those same lords were vassals of kings who many times despotically ruled their people; and the corrupt Catholic Church stood above them all as the de facto force to be reckoned with on all matters spiritual and temporal.[2] People across Europe had been grumbling for centuries under the injustices they endured, with even good Catholics like the famed Erasmus of Rotterdam noting the

---

1. Kolb, *Martin Luther*, 20.
2. Philpott, "Religious Roots," 21.

need for a move away from the folly and corruption that had beset the Church and society.³

Change was clearly needed, but even those who were critical of this corruption did not know quite how to effect such change. Loud voices such as John Hus, John Wycliffe, and others had denounced the corrupt practices and circumspect theology of the Church only to be branded as heretics and, in the case of Hus (and many of the followers of Wycliffe), burned at the stake. Clearly, a different type of change agent was needed if the powerful pope was to be ousted from his seat of authority.

LUTHER AS A CHANGE AGENT

Luther was the consummate change agent that had been needed for so long in Europe. Looking back on his accomplishments today, we can see a mosaic of societal changes that were introduced by Luther. But from a leadership studies perspective, it is important not just to describe these changes, but also analyze why Luther, in particular, was able to create such changes in the first place. In evaluating why he was so effective, this author has chosen to utilize John Kotter's (1996) model of change from his book *Leading Change*.⁴ Scholars have been studying change for thousands of years and have created myriad theories of change,⁵ but the simplicity and applicability of Kotter's model has made it a hallmark for leadership scholars in the last two decades. Kotter was influenced by a simple, yet profound model of change first developed by Kurt Lewin in 1951.⁶ Lewin had argued that, in order to effect change, a leader must take three steps: (1) unfreeze the status quo, (2) initiate the change, and (3) establish stability by refreezing the change as the new status quo. What Kotter did some forty-five years later was to expand this theory to explain how a leader actually engages in these three activities. His model includes eight steps

---

3. Montover, "Political and Temporal Dimensions," 124–33.

4. Kotter, *Leading Change*.

5. For instance, the ancient Greek, Hericlitus, believed that the natural state of the world was one of constant flux. His later Greek successor, Aristotle, wrote about change in his *Metaphysics* and how change from potentiality to actuality was a key driver in making robust systems. Much later, German writers such as Hegel and Marx saw a dialectic throughout history creating changes in society, and Charles Darwin, writing in the mid-1800s created a theory of evolution that was seen by many as a key indicator that only the most adaptable and change-oriented members of society could survive. In the last century, leadership scholars have written a broad array of works about different aspects of change, even going so far as to apply theories from the world of science to note how chaos and adaptability can be harnessed by effective leaders.

6. Lewin, *Field Theory*.

Section 2: Assessing Martin Luther's Leadership

that he believed were vital for good change leadership: (1) establish a sense of urgency; (2) create a guiding coalition; (3) develop a vision; (4) communicate the vision; (5) empower action by followers; (6) generate short-term wins; (7) consolidate gains and produce more change; and (8) cement new changes in the culture.[7] While Kotter's change model is geared toward an organizational setting, it can be adapted as a tool to examine societal change, as well. In so doing, some of Kotter's concepts must bend slightly toward a broader cultural context, but the robust nature of the theory still proves to be effective for the leadership scholar in analyzing societal change.

Kotter's change model begins by noting that a leader must establish a sense of urgency by ridding the group of complacency and creating a message that is communicated thoroughly to all followers. This urgency must be espoused, Kotter argues, not only by a relative few, but by a "guiding coalition" made up of key personnel—not just those with high positions, but those who are widely respected and admired by all.[8] Kotter relates that the change must be founded upon a central vision: one that appeals broadly to most of the people and which has its roots in improving the lot of the entire group.[9] But having a vision is not enough; Kotter notes that a guiding coalition's vision must be effectively communicated to all levels of the group. This must be done in a simple, easy-to-understand manner that uses many types of forums/platforms.[10]

While these first four steps of Kotter's model are about unfreezing the status quo, the remaining four steps of his model show how to initiate the change and refreeze it as the new status quo for the group. In his fifth step, Kotter argues that leaders must empower their subordinates to enact the desired change by stripping away structural barriers, providing training on how to implement the change, and creating systems that reward compliance with the vision for change.[11] But, Kotter notes, even the most passionate change agents in a group will lose their sense of empowerment if there are no definable results on the horizon. Kotter, therefore, implores leaders to create strategic "short-term wins" that can provide an infusion of energy and momentum.[12] Such recognizable goals are key to fostering a can-do attitude within the group, but the leader must not allow these small wins to thrust the group back into complacency. Thus, the leader must work hard to consolidate

7. Kotter, *Leading Change*, 21.
8. Ibid., 57.
9. Ibid., 73.
10. Ibid., 81–83.
11. Ibid., 103–10.
12. Ibid., 122.

gains, continue to produce more change, and finally, cement the change in the culture.

Establishing a Sense of Urgency

In applying Kotter's theory to Martin Luther, we start with Luther's ability to create a sense of urgency. As was discussed previously, the Catholic Church at the time was a behemoth, and taking it on was truly a David versus Goliath type of scenario. Previous radicals had largely failed in their efforts to end the rampant corruption in the Church, as the Church was simply too powerfully entrenched as the status quo in society. That Luther ever dared to step forth and proclaim a similar message at all was a sheer act of heroism in the face of almost certain death.[13]

One of the things that made Luther different from the Pre-Reformers was that he created a sense of urgency that was not just theological, but practical in nature. For more than half a century, the German people and their clergy had been complaining about the economic burdens the pope was exacting upon them.[14] High taxes, corruption, and the rampant selling of indulgences to pay for the construction of St. Peter's Basilica in Rome proved to be a crushing weight on the people of Germany. Nobles and peasants alike felt bruised from the economic blows that the Church kept leveling against them over and over. As Roland Bainton remarked, Germany had essentially become the pope's "private cow," one which he exploited many times over.[15]

Luther tapped into this feeling of German nationalism and highlighted the economic abuses against the people in his famous *95 Theses* and later writings.[16] But unlike previous leaders, who had focused solely on theological issues or practical issues in isolation, Luther masterfully welded the two together to create a sense of urgency.[17] Whereas previous calls for reform

---

13. Lawson, "Mighty Fortress," 26.
14. Montover, "Political and Temporal Dimensions," 124.
15. Bainton, *Here I Stand*, 122.
16. Ibid. An example of this can be found in his *Open Letter to the Christian Nobility*, written in 1520: "And they [the pope and his Italian clerics] all lie in wait for the prebends and benefices of Germany as wolves lie in wait for the sheep. I believe that Germany now gives much more to the pope at Rome than it gave in former times to the emperors. Indeed, some estimate that every year more than three hundred thousand gulden find their way from Germany to Rome, quite uselessly and fruitlessly; we get nothing for it but scorn and contempt. And yet we wonder that princes, nobles, cities, endowments, land and people are impoverished! We should rather wonder that we still have anything to eat!" (*LW* 44:142).
17. Montover, "Political and Temporal Dimensions," 124.

Section 2: Assessing Martin Luther's Leadership

had been primarily geared toward the clergy or the laity as separate entities, Luther broke these distinctions by arguing that each Christian was a part of the "priesthood of believers," able to go directly to God, decide his own conscience, and stand up against papal abuses.[18] On a theological level, Luther's arguments stripped away the authority of the clergy to stand as a barrier to God, allowing believers to have direct access to their Lord. But he did not stop there; on a very pragmatic level, tracts such as his *Open Letter to the Christian Nobility*, *On Secular Authority*, and others opened the way for the German people and temporal authorities to shake off the shackles of papal dominance. As Montover noted about Luther's concept of the priesthood of all believers:

> [Luther's] universal priesthood functioned as a fundamental attack on the medieval cosmology which was the root of papal claims of authority in the temporal sphere. His articulation of the universal priesthood prior to his calls for secular reform had the effect of dismantling all that stood in the way of the success of other reform movements. After tearing down the cosmology of his day, he was then able to consider the best way to rebuild the structures of his day.[19]

By wrapping practical concerns around a theological doctrine, Luther was thus able to create a sense of urgency in Germany that had not existed before. No longer was the issue merely economic in nature, or merely spiritual in nature. Instead, Luther's doctrine of the priesthood of all believers opened the eyes of nobles and peasants alike to the fact that they could do something about the grave abuses the pope had exacted against them. By fighting against spiritual oppression as well as economic oppression, Luther laid the groundwork for the people to see the need to "unthaw" the hardened status quo.

---

18. "How then if they are forced to admit that we are all equally priests, as many of us as are baptized, and by this way we truly are; while to them is committed only the Ministry (ministerium Predigtamf) and consented to by us (nosfro consensu)? If they recognize this they would know that they have no right to exercise power over us (ius imperii, in what has not been committed to them) except insofar as we may have granted it to them, for thus it says in 1 Peter 2, 'You are a chosen race, a royal priesthood, a priestly kingdom.' In this way we are all priests, as many of us as are Christians. There are indeed priests whom we call ministers. They are chosen from among us, and who do everything in our name. That is a priesthood which is nothing else than the Ministry. Thus 1 Corinthians 4:1: "No one should regard us as anything else than ministers of Christ and dispensers of the mysteries of God" (*LW* 36:112–13).

19. Montover, "Political and Temporal Dimensions," 133.

Develop a Guiding Coalition

Another key factor in Luther's success as a change agent was his guiding coalition of Reformers. Whereas other Pre-Reformers such as Wycliffe and Hus had engendered substantial followings among the laity, Luther was different in that he was able to foster a guiding coalition that included rich and poor, powerful and humble alike. His friends and followers hailed from the elite nobility, to theologians, city leaders, and peasants.[20] This guiding coalition made it practically possible for Luther to survive and create the momentum needed to enact the types of reforms that had failed before.

One of the most important parts of this guiding coalition was Luther's relationship to powerful princes. Never before had reformers had the backing of mighty political figures, and their patronage allowed Luther to first dodge the grasp of the pope and later cement reform into the structural beams of the culture. Early in Luther's career as a reformer, Frederick the Wise of Saxony was vitally important in keeping Luther alive.[21] In 1521, after several years of polemic writing by Luther, Charles V, the Holy Roman Emperor, had had enough. At the Diet of Worms, Charles had declared Luther an outlaw, which meant that, on a practical level, Luther was literally outside the protections of the law. Like other outlaws, this meant that he could be beaten, robbed, or killed without recourse to the traditional laws against assault, battery, or murder.[22] Obviously, this placed Luther in grave danger. Yet on Luther's way home from the Diet, Frederick, who was the powerful ruler of the territory of Saxony, devised a plan to keep Luther safe.[23] While travelling back to Wittenberg, Frederick had his men dress as bandits, pretend to kidnap Luther, and take him to one of Frederick's nearby castles. For close to a year, Frederick hid Luther in his Wartburg Castle, even going so far as to give him a fake name and have him grow out a beard so he would not be recognized. This period served as an incredibly profitable, though dreary, time for Luther: he was able to translate the entire New Testament into the German vernacular for the first time, develop his theology further, and prepare for his next steps in the Reformation movement.[24] But most importantly, this ruse allowed Luther to stay alive at a critical juncture in the Reformation. Had he died, the Reformation may never have gotten off the ground. By saving his life and putting him under his personal protection, Frederick served as the first of Luther's powerful

20. Kolb, *Martin Luther*, 20.
21. Bainton, *Here I Stand*, 122.
22. Kurtz, *Church History*, 123.
23. Kittelson and Wiersma, *Luther the Reformer*, 163.
24. Ibid., 175.

Section 2: Assessing Martin Luther's Leadership

friends who enabled him to have the protection to openly criticize the most powerful institution in the world at the time: the Catholic Church.

But Luther's guiding coalition did not just include a sole prince; Luther was able to cultivate important relationships with other nobles, city leaders, and theologians, as well.[25] In particular, Luther developed a network of important thinkers, writers, and activists within academia. Men such as Philip Melanchthon, Johannes Brenz, Martin Bucer, Andreas Osiander, Johann Oldendorp, and Johannes Bugenhagen, who were all professors at Wittenberg or nearby universities, served important roles in helping to propagate the Reformation's ideas.[26] Alongside Luther, these professors influenced the minds of thousands of students who would help to spread the ideas of Protestantism. But this group went further, as they also became actively involved in converting important nobles to Protestantism, serving as advisors to cities that had adopted Protestantism, and drafting new laws to help cities and territories truly reform all aspects of society. Drafting these new laws, in particular, had a broad-ranging impact, as dozens of cities and territories across Germany and Scandinavia began to adopt laws that were either directly written by, or inspired largely upon the writings of Luther, Melanchthon, and other notable Reformers.[27]

---

25. Manetsch, "Man in the Middle," 213–34.

26. Kittelson and Wiersma, *Luther the Reformer*, 185; Witte, *Law and Protestantism*, 15.

27. Witte, *Law and Protestantism*, 189–90, notes that "Luther himself helped to draft the new laws of Leisnig (1523) and Wittenberg (1533 and 1545), and also influenced the reformation ordinances of Gottingen (1530) and Herzberg (1538). Melanchthon's ideas dominated the new reformation laws of Nuremberg (1525), Wittenberg (1533), Herzberg (1538), Cologne (1543), and Meckenburg (1552) and also lay at the heart of the territorial laws of Hesse (1526) and Saxony (1533). Melanchthon also had considerable influence on legal reforms in Tubingen, Frankfurt an der Oder, Leipzig, Rostock, Heidelberg, Marburg, and Jena. Johannes Brenz helped to draft the early reformation laws of Schwabisch-Hall (1526 and 1543) and Brandenburg-Nurnberg (1533) and was the principal draftsman of the massive reformation ordinances of Wurttemberg (1536, 1537, 1553, 1556, 1559). Justus Jonas had a strong influence on the reformation ordinances of Wittenberg (1533, 1545), Saxony (1538), and Halle (1541). Andreas Osiander played a crucial role in negotiating and promulgating the reformation laws of Brandenburg (1533) and Pfalzneuburg (1543). Johann Oldendorp helped to shape the reformation laws of Rostock (1530). . . . Martin Bucer had a strong hand in drafting the new laws of Strasbourg (1524), and Ulm (1531) and also influenced the new reformation laws of Augsburg (1537), Kassel (1539), and Cologne (1543). . . . Bugenhagen drafted the city reformation laws of Brunswick (1528 and 1543), Hamburg (1529), Lubeck (1531), Bremen (1534), and Hildensheim (1544). He also had a strong hand in drafting the laws for the territories of Pomerania (1535), Schleswig-Holstein (1542), Brunswick-Wolfenbuttel (1543), and the Kingdoms of Norway and Denmark (1537)."

Luther cultivated close relationships with these individuals over time, and the dividends were immense. By having a guiding coalition of prominent men throughout Germany who were spreading his ideas, Luther was able to multiply his efforts tenfold from what he would have been able to accomplish by himself. Likewise, men like Martin Bucer and Johannes Bugenhagen eventually travelled to England, Denmark, and Sweden, helping to spread the Reformation outside of Germany. Luther's guiding coalition was thus immensely important in spreading his vision and creating the laws and social structures that would eventually cement that vision into the culture.

Design and Create a Vision

One of the most unique characteristics of Martin Luther as a change agent was that he formed a vision for the Reformation that included not only theological concerns, but the reformation of all of society.[28] Theologically, his vision was guided by the five *solas*: (1) *sola fide* (salvation is by faith alone); (2) *sola scriptura* (the Bible is the ultimate authority for Christians); (3) *sola gratia* (God saves sinners by his grace alone); (4) *solus Christus* (Christ is Lord and the only path to salvation); and (5) *soli deo gloria* (Christians are to live to the glory of God alone).[29] While these doctrines provided a comprehensive and sweeping theological shift from Catholicism, Luther did not develop this theological vision overnight. Instead, Luther was persuaded over time by what he saw in the Scriptures. As early as 1517, Luther's 95 *Theses* were primarily concerned with the spiritual and economic corruption found in the sale of indulgences by the Church. But over time, his reading of the Bible caused him to continue to broaden his theology outside of traditional Catholic norms. The doctrines he developed during this theological journey had an important role in laying the spiritual and intellectual foundation for change in society. In contrast to Catholic theology, Luther's theology focused on God's grace, man's salvation through faith rather than works, the authority of the Bible, the centrality of Christ, and a life lived in direct relationship to God and for his glory alone.[30]

But this new theology did not just change the vision for the spiritual side of society; instead, Luther believed this new theology touched every sphere of the culture. As I have discussed in my previous chapter on Luther's impact on politics, education, the law, and economics, Luther's vision touched almost

---

28. Bainton, *Here I Stand*, 233.
29. Sproul, *Legacy of Luther*.
30. Ibid.; Bainton, *Here I Stand*.

Section 2: Assessing Martin Luther's Leadership

every area of society. From new laws, to new ways of seeing the prince, to new ways of seeing education and poor relief, Luther's and his colleagues' vision had such a broad ranging scope that it was not merely limited to the spiritual lives of Protestant followers. Instead, it was a transformational vision that viewed God's sovereignty as being over all areas of life.[31] This holistic vision was unique in that it did not just promise to change the spiritual lives of the people, but their whole culture.

Communicate the Vision

While Luther's vision for Protestantism was quite compelling and revolutionary, it likely would not have had a large impact had he not also been effective in communicating the vision to his people. Luther's movement for reform happened to coincide with an explosion in printing in the early 1500s in Germany.[32] Before the 1440s, when a German inventor named Johannes Gutenberg created the first moveable type printing press in the West, books and tracts had been difficult to reproduce to a large audience. But by the time of Luther, printing presses had sprung up all over Germany, and they needed content to sell. Luther's revolutionary ideas coupled with his easy-to-understand writing style made for an ideal match. It also did not hurt that Luther's writing was voluminous and touched a broad cross-section of topics that would interest readers across social strata.[33] From the beginning, printers created broadsheets showing snippets of his writings, tracts, pamphlets, whole editions of his works, and more. Likewise, because there were no other forms of mass visual media, many aspiring printers, authors, and artists created woodcuts of Luther's profile, short biographies of his life, and images of his famous battles against the pope. These images, broadsides, tracts, and books spread like wildfire and had the effect of making Luther an overnight hero for the German people. Like no one before him, his courageous stand, heartfelt convictions, strong theology, and deep love for the plight of the German people made his works the talk of the nation. It is estimated that, during his lifetime, a full 20 percent of the works printed in Germany were either written by Luther or

---

31. "Thus it has come about that men are saying to the pope and his followers, Tu ora, 'Thou shalt pray'; to the emperor and his followers, Tu protege, 'Thou shalt guard'; to the common man, Tu 1abora, 'Thou shalt work.' Not, however, as though everyone were not to pray, guard and work; for the man who is diligent in his calling is praying, guarding and working in all that he does" (*LW* 44:156).
32. Kolb, *Martin Luther*, 20.
33. Becker, "Causes and Consequences," 16–17.

were about him.[34] He came to have almost rockstar status among Germans as he served as one of the first national heroes for his people.[35] From 1517 till his death, Luther wrote dozens of works in a steady stream that kept the people enthralled with him and his message of reform.

From a leadership perspective, this high volume of communication was of paramount importance for the acceptance of Luther's vision for change.[36] In writing about communication, Kotter notes that effective change agents must communicate their vision in practical and symbolic ways through a variety of mediums and in a steady stream of communications over time.[37] Luther provides a textbook case of how this was done for an entire people group. Over the course of several decades, he dominated the printing market to such an extent that almost every literate German had likely read or heard of his works.[38] Likewise, the plethora of images of his heroic stands against the pope and illustrations about his theological works helped even the illiterate in society gain an understanding of what his vision encompassed.[39] He made sure to produce works continuously over time, and at the urging of many other leaders, wrote about a variety of topics that were germane to his initiative for reform. As Luther himself noted: "God's highest and ultimate gift of grace by which He would have His Gospel carried forward."[40]

Not only did Luther produce a great amount of work, but his colleagues and students also disseminated his message widely through their own works. Melanchthon, Bucer, Bugenhagen, and others produced their own important works that helped to undergird Luther's message.[41] Likewise, many other Protestant scholars within Luther's network began producing works that explained and expanded on his views in areas such as law, education, and economics. Luther's students also took copious notes of his lectures and private dinner conversations, which they compiled into a compendium called *Table Talk* after his death.[42] Because this guiding coalition of followers also produced a

---

34. Kolb, *Martin Luther*, 19.
35. Kittelson and Wiersma, *Luther the Reformer*, 228; Kolb, *Martin Luther*, 26.
36. Bainton, *Here I Stand*, 302.
37. Kotter, *Leading Change*, 87.
38. "The printed word played a crucial role in the early Reformation, and when multiplied by the effects of preaching and conversation, can be said to be a major factor in spreading a relatively coherent message throughout German-speaking lands." Kolb, *Martin Luther*, 19, quoting Edwards, *Printing Propaganda*, 172.
39. Ibid., 26–31.
40. Bainton, *Here I Stand*, 302.
41. Witte, *Law and Protestantism*.
42. Bainton, *Here I Stand*, 305.

great volume of literature for the masses, Luther's message of change reached even more people than if he had been a solitary individual writing by himself.

Empower Action by Followers

While communicating a compelling vision is vital for the success of any change initiative, leaders must also strip away barriers to change that impede the growth of the movement.[43] Likewise, not only must those leaders strip away old barriers, but they must construct new systems that encourage others to align themselves with the change initiative.[44] For Luther, this meant a two-pronged attack on not only the Catholic Church, but its grip on societal institutions. By the 1500s, the Catholic Church dominated not only the spiritual lives of the populous, but also the economic, legal, political, and cultural spheres of Western society. As Luther developed his theology over time, he saw that the pope's corrupt influence on all areas of society had led to decay in both the Church and society. Thus, he began to attack not only the theological beliefs that undergirded the pope's authority, but also the monastic and ecclesiastical institutions that helped the pope dominate all areas of society.

But unlike many before and after him, Luther was not merely a critic; he was also a visionary architect for society. Through his writings, peasants and princes alike started to see that a reformation in all spheres of Western culture was truly possible. Luther and his fellow Reformers did not just offer criticism of papal institutions, but provided solutions for how Protestant territories could create more God-honoring institutions. As noted previously, these suggestions soon became model laws that were adopted by dozens of cities, territories, and nations.[45] From a leadership perspective, these new laws broke down the barriers to change and provided a new structural edifice for Protestant societies.

Generate Short-Term Wins

While the new laws and structural edifices that Luther and his colleagues developed over time were important, they may never have come to fruition if the Reformation had not generated several important short-term wins. Almost any change movement will fail if followers do not see marked progress in the short run, and thus it is imperative that leaders generate practical and symbolic

43. Kotter, *Leading Change*, 103–10.
44. Ibid.
45. Berman, "Spiritualization of Secular Law," 317.

victories in the early stages of the change movement.[46] The Reformation had just these types of important short-term wins in the early years. As mentioned previously, one of Luther's first victories was in securing the powerful protection of Frederick the Wise. This alliance very likely saved his life, and gave him time to generate other key victories. During his time at the Wartburg Castle, Luther diligently worked on a translation of the New Testament into the vernacular German language. While this was an important symbolic step, the practical implications of this translation were immense. With this translation, Luther gave the German people the ability to go straight to the Scriptures themselves in their own language.[47] This was an important short-term win because it represented a practical application of Luther's theology in everyday life. Luther had been writing extensively about the idea of the priesthood of the believer, but up to this time, the German populous still could not access the Scriptures without the aid of a priest or someone else who knew how to read Latin. By diligently working to create a translation of the Scriptures into German, Luther was able to not just theologically, but also practically cut out people's total dependence on the clergy for their access to God.[48] Now, every man or woman who could read German could also read God's Word. While it took many years of Luther and others advocating for universal education so that every German could learn to read the Scriptures for themselves, Luther's early translation provided a short-term win that opened the promise of God's Word to everyone in Germany.[49]

Likewise, while Luther in the early years of the Reformation may have been more focused on spiritual matters, it did not hurt that his colleagues and followers were busy collecting short-term wins by convincing cities, towns, and territories to adopt Protestant teachings.[50] These early adopters created momentum for the new movement and showed that the movement had staying power. As Luther and the Reformation faced increasing attacks from the Catholic Church and powerful rulers within Germany itself, these Protestant cities, towns, and territories became an important network that allowed the movement to protect itself and continue to spread.[51] As more and more short-

46. Kotter, *Leading Change*, 121.
47. Berman, "Spiritualization of Secular Law," 319–20.
48. Becker and Woessmann, "Was Weber Wrong?," 8.
49. Lawson, "Mighty Fortress," 39.
50. Witte, *Law and Protestantism*, 189–91.

51. While this network symbolically gave legitimacy to the Reformation, it also had a practical benefit. By the early 1530s, Protestant princes were sensing a need for military protection against powerful Catholic stalwarts, and formed this loose network of Protestant cities and territories into what became known as the Schmalkaldic League, a defensive alliance that helped preserve the ability of the fledgling movement to grow.

Section 2: Assessing Martin Luther's Leadership

term wins piled up for the Reformation, other cities and territories, including the nations of Denmark and Sweden, began to follow suit and adopt Luther's teachings. But the spread of this movement may have stalled early on had some of the early adoption cities never taken the proverbial leap of faith to publicly accept Luther's teachings.

Consolidating Improvements and Cementing Change in the Culture

As the Reformation began to take hold in Germany and beyond, Luther and his colleagues took important steps to consolidate change and cement that change in the culture. One of their most important tools in this cause was the power of their voluminous writings. During his lifetime, Luther alone wrote hundreds of works on matters ranging from theology, to trade, education, the law, and more. With the power of the printing press adding exposure, Luther's writings became influential treatises that informed many areas of life in Protestant lands. Similarly, colleagues of Luther such as Philip Melanchthon wrote extensively across a broad range of topics, and these writings similarly ingrained Protestant ideals into the minds and hearts of the populous.[52]

In addition to theological, legal, and other treatises, Luther and other Reformers also began to write hymns as a way to teach laypeople about basic doctrine. Luther in particular saw the need to inculcate the laity through a variety of mediums so that the truths of the Bible would sink into their hearts and minds.[53] These early hymns, which were specifically written for the first time in German so that the people could sing them, served as important tools in helping Protestant clergy teach their parishioners about key biblical concepts.[54]

In a similar vein, Luther himself penned a *Small Catechism* that was meant to provide even young people with the key doctrinal concepts they would need to be productive members of the Church and their communities.[55] Later, Luther also drafted a *Large Catechism* that served as a more broad-based tool to help members of the congregation dive deeper in their understanding of God's truths. When coupled with the hymns he produced, these catechisms

---

Shortly after Luther's death, the alliance became a necessity for Protestant lands as the Catholic rulers fought Protestant princes in what came to be known as the Schmalkaldic War. Methuen, *Luther and Calvin*, 52.

52. Witte, *Law and Protestantism*, 15.
53. Kittelson and Wiersma, *Luther the Reformer*, 219.
54. Lawson, "Mighty Fortress," 47.
55. Kittelson and Wiersma, *Luther the Reformer*, 217.

served as important tools for cementing the Reformation's key doctrines into the minds and hearts of the general public.[56]

Likewise, Luther and others advocated strongly for universal education for both boys and girls in order to not only make them good citizens, but also help them learn how to read the Bible for themselves.[57] More than almost anything else Luther did as a leader, his push for educational reform had one of the most broad-ranging impacts on all areas of society.[58] From politics, to commerce, the law, and social structures, the ripple effects of universal education ranged far and wide. Luther wrote for decades about the priesthood of the believer, but it was his educational reforms that gave legs to this doctrine in a practical sense. For if regular people could not read God's Word for themselves, how were they to operate as a priesthood of believers? By advocating for the education of the populace, Luther and others cemented their doctrinal changes into the very fabric of Protestant society, allowing good German Protestants to exercise their "priestly" duties in applying God's commands in all spheres of life.[59]

While these methodical measures may not have been as awe-inspiring as other acts that Luther took, they were important measures that helped to consolidate and cement the change he had initiated in 1517. Over time, Protestant Christians began to have the education and theological training they needed to truly serve as the priesthood of believers that Luther felt they were all called to be. These shifts ingrained Protestantism not just in the theology of the culture, but in the very fabric of society. Because of this, Luther left his lasting legacy not only in the courageous stands he took as a young man, but in his dedicated advocacy over many decades on behalf of the education and inculcation of the German people in God's truths.

---

56. Hendrix, "Luther's Impact."

57. "Above all, the foremost and most general subject of study, both in the higher and the lower schools, should be the Holy Scriptures, and for the young boys the Gospel. And would to God that every town had a girls' school also, in which the girls were taught the Gospel for an hour each day either in German or Latin" (*LW* 44:205–6); "If then there were no soul, as I have said, and if there were no need at all of schools and languages for the sake of the Scriptures and of God, this one consideration should suffice to establish everywhere the very best schools for both boys and girls, namely, that in order outwardly to maintain its temporal estate, the world must have good and skilled men and women, so that the former may rule well over land and people and the latter may keep house and train children and servants aright" (*LW* 45:368).

58. Kittelson and Wiersma, *Luther the Reformer*, 243.

59. Becker and Woessmann, "Was Weber Wrong?," 4.

Section 2: Assessing Martin Luther's Leadership

CONCLUSION

While the 1500s may seem like ancient history to many modern leaders, there is much that we can learn from Martin Luther and his success as a change agent. Whereas others before him had called for reform, it was Luther who was able to put all the pieces together to create a reformation movement that truly transformed society. He did not do this wholly by himself, but built a sense of urgency alongside a guiding coalition of like-minded Reformers. As their ideas coalesced into a true vision for change which they communicated through a variety of mediums, these Protestant Reformers sparked a change movement that touched all areas of society. But as with any change initiative, their efforts to empower others, generate short-term wins, consolidate gains, and cement the change in the culture were equally as important. Luther shined as a change agent because he doggedly pursued this vision over three decades and beckoned others to come along with him. In the Protestant West, we can be eternally grateful that this man of many talents was not only a great theologian, but also the ideal change agent for his time.

6

Luther as an Adaptive Leader

Dr. Erik Gronberg

Martin Luther lived in a tumultuous and dramatic time in the history of Western Europe. New ideas about the nature of the individual, rising national interests, and contact with new worlds and other faiths were challenging the dominance of the Holy Roman Empire and the Roman Catholic Hierarchy. In this tumult, Luther recognized and seized the opportunity to become a significant leadership figure in the history of the Western world.

The chapter will demonstrate how Luther utilized traits of adaptive leadership both during the reformation moment in 1517 but also after when he fully realized the adaptive challenge at hand. Without the assumption of papal and church authority a question arose as to who had authority to step in and teach, preach, and provide advice to pastors and lay leaders. This chapter will demonstrate that Luther did so, along with his followers, in order that the church might continue to have an efficacious role in the life of the people. In so doing he sets an example for current day church leaders challenged to teach and pass on the faith.

INTRODUCTION

Ronald Heifetz's publication of *Leadership Without Easy Answers* in 1994 has led to the growth of adaptive leadership into a widely recognized and significant leadership concept and theory. Adaptive leadership, as defined by

Section 2: Assessing Martin Luther's Leadership

Heifetz, begins with the leader's acknowledgment that the existing framework of the context provides no obvious solution to the presenting issue.[1] The leader then must draw together individuals (followers) to find a new pathway to a solution. This sort of leadership requires experimentation, risk of failure, and new learning on the part of leader and follower.[2] In organizations or institutions, a crisis often creates the situation or opportunity where adaptive leadership is required.

Martin Luther and his community faced such a significant crisis in the early part of the sixteenth century. Luther's dramatic challenge to the status quo, begun with the posting and publication of the 95 *Theses*, a technical response to the challenge he saw, created a situation that this chapter will demonstrate required adaptive responses. Yet by publishing his theses, it is clear that he initially thought that he could address his mounting concerns about the church's ministry through the technical structures of the church.

Luther had been taught many tools in his academic and ecclesial career and as such was not unfounded in his belief that such tools would work. As a result, he began his reformation career with academic theses and debate based on scriptural evidence and appeals to tradition.[3] However, this chapter will demonstrate that Luther would quickly come to understand the leadership context in which he was working and that the hierarchy who made the rules was decidedly not in favor of such a solution.

As a leader Luther would have to learn along with his followers what it meant to move outside of the hierarchy of the church to find new solutions to the crisis. In so doing he would come to challenge the existing ecclesial and theological structure, become deeply entwined into local and international politics, as well as ultimately be part of creating a new community of believers. This community ultimate would, against his desire, take the name Lutheran and continue his theological legacy for the next five hundred years.

Luther had, by design or accident, become a change agent. This new role would then require of him to find new and significant ways to relate to followers. These followers were not always ready to simply follow him into the unknown. This community of believers had come to depend on the structure for organizing their lives and their faith. Luther had disrupted this structure,

---

1. Heifetz, *Leadership without Easy Answers*, 100.
2. Heifetz et al., *Adaptive Leadership*, 14–17.
3. Luther, *Theological Writings*, 14; Nestingen, *Martin Luther*, 26–29. In both the 95 *Theses* and the Heidelberg Disputation, Luther can be seen as still attempting to work through the machinery of the church. He assumed that once the hierarchy was aware, they would correct the abuses.

challenged the status quo, and would need to learn how to be a leader in the liminal context in which he was living and had helped to create.

To accomplish these tasks, this chapter argues that Luther would need to exercise the leadership traits of what today would be identified as the toolbox of the adaptive leader. In addition to exercising these traits, this chapter will also argue that indeed he was successful in that enterprise. However, to understand what labeling him as an adaptive leader means a brief introduction to adaptive leadership theory is required.

ADAPTIVE LEADERSHIP AS THEORY

Adaptive leadership theory is based on the foundational work of Ronald Heifetz who defined the theory of adaptive leadership over and against what he referred to as technical leadership.[4] Technical leadership works when solutions to the problem are evident and the challenge can be solved by providing previously established tools, technology, or by learning how to better motivate individuals.[5]

Technical leadership assumes the leader can provide the path to the solution. However, often times this solution is incomplete and may resolve the symptoms of the leadership challenge but fails to address the root cause. This root cause is often structural challenges that prevent the technical solution from being fully effective. Ultimately, identifying, analyzing, and diagnosing the system is the adaptive challenge. The leader must identify the adaptive challenge. New learning and new negotiation of the authority and practice of leadership will be required.[6]

---

4. Heifetz, *Leadership without Easy Answers*, 100; Heifetz et al., *Adaptive Leadership*, 14.

5. Bass, *Handbook*, 27–29; Heifetz et al., *Adaptive Leadership* 70.

6. Bass, *Handbook*, 354–59; Heifetz, *Leadership without Easy Answers*, 71–76; Heifetz and Laurie, "Work of Leadership," 5–15.

Section 2: Assessing Martin Luther's Leadership

Table 1. Leadership with Authority in Adaptive Situation

Social Function	Situational Type	
	Technical	Adaptive
Direction	Authority provides problem definition and solution	Authority identifies the adaptive challenge, provides diagnosis of condition, and produces questions about problem definitions and solutions
Protection	Authority protects from external threat	Authority discloses external threat
Role Orientation	Authority orients	Authority disorients current roles, or resists pressure to orient people in new roles too quickly.
Controlling Conflict	Authority restores order	Authority exposes conflict, or lets it emerge
Norm Maintenance	Authority maintains norms	Authority challenges norms, or allows them to be challenged

Source: **Heifetz, Leadership without Easy Answers, 127.**

The leader in a technical situation is clearly in control, retains power, and is even dominant over followers. Adaptive situations create an environment where leadership is much more of a negotiation. Adaptive leaders must recognize the leader's job is not to provide direction, comfort, security, control conflict, or to maintain the status quo. Instead, the adaptive leader must challenge social norms and will create disorientation for the community to engage in new learning. The adaptive leader, as a result, must be willing to challenge and disorient followers, disclose threats, and challenge norms, traits that Martin Luther certainly had.

Heifetz identifies three types of situations requiring leadership and table 2 outlines them utilizing a medical decision process as the guide. Drawing on the adaptive and technical types identified in table 1, Heifetz outlines three situations and demonstrates the conditions that generate the need to make a shift from technical leadership into the kind of work required for adaptive leadership.

Table 2. Three Types of Situations

Situation	Problem definition	Solution and implementation	Primary locus of responsibility for the work	Kind of work
Type I	Clear	Clear	Physician	Technical
Type II	Clear	Requires learning	Physician and patient	Technical and adaptive
Type III	Requires learning	Requires learning	Patient > physician	Adaptive

Source: **Heifetz, Leadership without Easy Answers, 76.**

Heifetz recognizes the multiple challenges of adaptive leadership. The primary challenge is that this sort of leadership requires experimentation and learning. Experimentation, he admits, will lead to failures and new discoveries. The learning will require the adjustment of attitudes for individuals and groups and also lead to anxiety. Unfortunately, he acknowledges failure may not be acceptable to individuals or large groups of people and the leader may face significant opposition or even attempts at assassination.[7]

Adaptive work requires the leader to step back and both assess the situation and challenge followers. This leadership is focused less on the leader's personal qualities as on their actions in relationship to their followers. The leader must give the work back to the group to think critically and discern the proper direction for the organization. Heifetz argues this sort of learning leadership can and will produce better results.[8] However, in a less transparent or mature situation, the followers may rebel against the leader for failing to provide expected comfort. To be an effective adaptive leader Heifetz offers five key themes.[9]

1. Identify the adaptive challenge.
2. Keep the level of distress within a tolerable range for doing adaptive work.
3. Focus attention on ripening issues not on stress reducing distractions.
4. Give the work back to the people.
5. Protect voices without authority.

---

7. Heifetz, *Leadership without Easy Answers*, 237–39; Heifetz et al., *Adaptive Leadership*, 283; Heifetz and Laurie, "Work of Leadership," 11.

8. Heifetz, *Leadership without Easy Answers*, 251–52; Heifetz et al., *Adaptive Leadership*, 105–7.

9. Heifetz, *Leadership without Easy Answers*, 128.

Section 2: Assessing Martin Luther's Leadership

These five principles demonstrate the importance of the relationship of leader and follower in adaptive leadership theory. The development and learning of followers is a vitally important goal of this leadership style.[10]

Political climates of decaying trust in hierarchical and institutional authority have changed the expectations of political leaders over the past several decades. In Luther's time, the secular and sacred hierarchy still held immense political and military power over and against their people. Yet they, too, were experiencing decaying levels of trust, radical changes in the economic systems of their time, and a growing unwillingness to simply accept authority. Luther's reforms were far from the only challenges to the established order in his time.[11] Ultimately this reality of the need for negotiating power between Emperor and the Princes was what kept Luther alive long enough to make his reforms known.

Leaders today and even in Luther's time are required and expected to do their work with and through the public. One of the goals of such political leadership should be in developing the people's ability to problem solve in community.[12] This again affirms that all leadership is learned and executed in context. Leaders operate along with and on behalf of followers. Good adaptive leadership requires making sure the right people are doing the right work.[13]

DOES THE THEORY APPLY?

Living in the first half of the sixteenth century, Martin Luther would not have been aware of leadership as an academic discipline and certainly not of the theory of adaptive leadership. However, this chapter is arguing Luther acted in ways that today would be understood as reflecting the traits of adaptive leadership. Adaptive leadership is both a prescriptive and descriptive theory. Knowledge of the theory is not a prerequisite of practicing its tenets.

To accomplish this goal, the chapter will focus on three examples of Luther's actions in specific leadership contexts. The focus will first be on the initial exciting moments of the Reformation in 1517 and the immediate years after. Luther's theological insights will be shown to in fact be an adaptive leadership move. The next two examples come from within the following decades. During this time, Luther demonstrated adaptive leadership as he helped build

---

10. Heifetz et al., *Adaptive Leadership*, 24; Heifetz and Linsky, *Leadership on the Line*, 14.

11. Nestingen, *Martin Luther*, 49, 57–58. The Peasants' War in 1525 is an example of this challenge.

12. Heifetz and Sinder, "Political Leadership," 200–202.

13. Ibid., 196.

a new church community and supported his followers. These examples will focus on his responses to the leadership gap in the communities and the lack of sufficient resources to equip followers to share their faith. The first of these two will be his work during the Saxon visitations in 1529 and his response to the concerns raised in those visits. The second will be the development of *The Small Catechism* in 1529, an adaptive teaching tool created to equip followers.

In these case studies, it will be shown that Luther was adept in recognizing the unique adaptive challenge of each situation. The status quo had been challenged and the institution as constructed was unable or unwilling to change. Even if the institution had been willing to change, the reality is it lacked the tools to do so. Changing expectations, new ideas, and rising nationalism made the church hierarchy unable to adapt quickly. Luther demonstrated that he was willing to learn, focused on his relationships with followers, and kept the focus on the main issues and avoided distractions.

Luther was focused not on the preservation of the institution but on the need for gospel proclamation and teaching for his followers. He also was deeply concerned for their physical, spiritual, and emotional needs. He quickly realized the need for pragmatic and realistic approaches to leading and teaching and responded quickly and effectively. Luther, through this adaptive leadership, ultimately set the stage for an entirely new way of thinking about the relationship of individuals to God and their church, as well as the form and function of how that gospel message was to be proclaimed.

THE REFORMATION "MOMENT"

On the eve of All Saints, 1517, a relatively unknown young professor of theology is said to have nailed his *95 Theses* upon the door of the Castle Church in Wittenberg, Germany. Since that time, many have debated whether he posted them physically on the door or posted them to the mail. Regardless of the method, October 31, 1517 has become a significant turning point in the history of Western Christendom and has become the "anniversary date" for the beginning of the Protestant Reformation.[14]

This 1517 reformation moment is important in an adaptive understanding of Luther's leadership because this moment precipitated and made necessary his acknowledgement of the adaptive challenge. Luther did not intend for these theses to be spread among lay Germans. In fact he made little effort to do so. As an academic, Luther knew how to use the tools of academic debate

---

14. Bainton, *Here I Stand*, 65; Nestingen, *Martin Luther*, 26; Lohrmann, *Book of Harmony*, 2; Nestingen, *Martin Luther*, 26.

Section 2: Assessing Martin Luther's Leadership

and inquiry to make his case. The purpose of his *95 Theses* was to press his case with the academic and ecclesial community. He desired to make the abuses of the indulgence sellers known to those who had the technical leadership authority to make changes. However, others found these theses provocative and shared them widely. As a result, Luther soon found that his profile was quickly being raised.[15]

Luther had a "love and zeal for the truth."[16] He firmly believed at this time that if only he could communicate to the proper authorities the abuses of the indulgence preachers, the situation would be solved. This line of thinking believed that surely Archbishop Albert of Mainz, and by extension the pope, was unaware of these abuses or else he would have already reigned in the sale of indulgences.[17] Luther's primary concern here, for the wellbeing of his followers, resonates with core tenets of adaptive leadership.

It did not take long for Luther and others to recognize that there was something more fundamentally wrong with the sale of indulgences and that those in positional authority were not inclined to make the changes he desired. In fact, he soon realized that what he had proposed would be challenging key doctrines and the very structure of the Roman Catholic Church.[18] This realization, coming in the months after the posting of the theses, led to his dramatic challenge to the basis of the church's teachings on sin and grace. This teaching continues as the basis for the confessions of what is today known as the Evangelical Lutheran Church.[19]

During this time, Luther came to more fully recognize this adaptive challenge and change he was pursuing. He was asked to give a lecture in April 1518 and he did not disappoint but prepared a make a dramatic statement in what became known as the Heidelberg Disputation. Luther did not equivocate despite the pressures being placed upon him from both Rome and his own elector, but argued for an end to the indulgences and a reliance on God's grace alone.

Working in a style that today could be recognized as adaptive leadership, he focused on the ripening issue and exposed the conflict rather than

---

15. Bainton, *Here I Stand*, 70.

16. Ibid., 54–55; *Theological Writings*, 4, 8. Luther did not move beyond technical solutions in this moment. However, his adaptive thinking did not just spring up either. It had been developing through his writings before 1517, particularly in his writings on the Psalms. Luther argued that the human will, which the scholastics argued was free, was in fact not free but that "humans are by nature unable to want God to be God. Indeed, they want to be God." Already Luther was changing the paradigm.

17. Bainton, *Here I Stand*, 71–72.

18. Nestingen, *Martin Luther*, 28–30.

19. Kolb and Wengert, *Book of Concord*.

attempted to cover it up. His proposal at the Heidelberg Disputation was an adaptive solution to the indulgence issue. The *theologica crucis* (theology of the cross) shifted the center and focus of the conversation about salvation.[20] This adaptive theological solution places God, not humanity, as the key subject in any sentence about salvation.[21] "The Law says, 'Do This,' and it is never done. Grace says 'Believe in this,' and everything is already done."[22] Luther, in this adaptive move, made fulfillment of the law not the requirement for salvation but the outcome of grace.

It is hard to overstate how radical Luther was articulating this theological understanding of the church and God's work in grace. It completely changed the nature of the salvation act by articulating a new way of understanding and proclaiming how God's grace worked in human salvation. In this way Luther proposed an adaptive solution to the age old question of how a human being was saved. This solution both decreased the anxiety of followers in their concerns about their own salvation, since that was God's gift to be give, as well as increased their responsibility to their neighbor in good works to be done in response to this gift of grace.

Luther, seeing his followers being led astray, led like Heifetz's classic example of a doctor who works with a terminal patient to create new meaning and purpose in a diagnosis.[23] Rather than simply apply more medicine (indulgences), he set his followers free to be servants to their neighbors out of love. His theology of the cross made God the subject of the salvation question and freed followers then to respond to God through works of righteousness done to earn God's grace but because God's grace had already freely been given.[24]

---

20. Lohrmann, *Book of Harmony*, 33–36; Luther, *Theological Writings*, 14.

21. Luther, *Theological Writings*, 120. Luther further developed this in his sermon in 1518 on Phil 2:5–6 entitled *The Two Kinds of Righteousness*. Here he speaks of God's "alien" righteousness that is instilled in human beings by grace alone. God acts first, humanity then responds to that grace by good works. This completely flipped the sixteenth-century understanding of salvation and the entire purpose for indulgences.

22. Ibid., 16.

23. Heifetz, *Leadership without Easy Answers*, 76–84. Heifetz used the example of a patient with a terminal diagnosis. The doctor (the leader) must look beyond technical medical options to help lead the patient and family (the followers) toward an outcome in which physical death occurs but the quality of what life remains is valued and meaning is found even in suffering.

24. Lohrmann, *Book of Harmony*, 35–36, 110–11; Luther, *Theological Writings*, 414. *Freedom of a Christian* articulates his understanding of a new paradigm of freedom and servanthood. "A Christian is servant of all and made subject to all. Insofar as a Christian is free, no works are necessary. Insofar as a Christian is a servant, all kinds of works are done."

Section 2: Assessing Martin Luther's Leadership

This new model put the needs of followers to know that God was for them first and focused them on key issues such as love for neighbor rather than self-serving distractions like indulgences. Luther was creating a holding environment for followers in which they could process God's grace for them and then be given the work of caring for their neighbor without guilt or fear. The challenge would now come from his followers who upon hearing of this freedom, of the gift of grace, began to overreact and take their freedom too far.

WORKING WITH FOLLOWERS: WITTENBERG (1521–22) AND SAXON VISITATIONS (1529)

Luther's teachings and unwillingness to recant at the Diet of Worms in 1521 created an unstable and occasionally violent situation in churches across Germany. This was even more the case in Wittenberg and the immediately surrounding areas. Some of Luther's followers, especially Andreas von Karlstadt, took his proclamation of freedom so far that they began to reject all of Roman practice and teaching. Confession was abandoned, church windows were broken, vestments, and other holy vessels were destroyed.[25]

Luther made a secret visit to Wittenberg in December of 1521, saw what was happening and was appalled. However, being hidden away limited his influence and his followers were unsure if he was even alive. Once more, Luther made an adaptive move and prepared a translation of the Bible into the German vernacular.[26] In so doing, he continued his adaptive work of disorienting current norms and exposing further conflict. A translation of the Scriptures out of the Latin would forever change the relationship of the churches taking part in the Reformation with Rome. It also served to give the work back to the people by providing them a copy of the Scriptures for their own reading. Additionally, this translation defined the German language for centuries to come.[27]

Upon arriving back in Wittenberg in 1522, at still some considerable risk to his personal safety, Luther fully realized how far things had gotten out of hand. Luther needed to provide some sort of stability as a leader. This is the adaptive key trait of creating a "holding environment" for followers. They needed to be assured that they were not being led astray but that they were being called into a new way of living and being. Immediately, Luther began a

---

25. Luther, *Theological Writings*, 289; Nestingen, *Martin Luther*, 48–49.
26. Bainton, *Here I Stand*, 336–39.
27. Nestingen, *Martin Luther*, 50–51.

series of daily sermons in which he pushed back against the radical leadership and took time to teach the people.[28]

Luther did not mince words and challenged the disorder of his followers. "Do not make a 'must' out of what is 'free'" was one of his key lines.[29] In these actions and statements, Luther was protecting his Wittenberg community and particularly those without authority. These were the lay people whom Luther had been so concerned about from the beginning. In these sermons and through his reigning in of the chaos he was creating a safe space for them and protecting them from leaders who would take the opportunity to simply become new dominating leaders and render the Reformation's focus on freedom null.

Luther also had an eye on the wider church at this time. Winning in Wittenberg was only one of his goals. He hoped that his Reformation movement and the understanding of the gospel that he was proclaiming would spread widely. He also knew that his protection, the princes who were both his followers and leaders, needed him to be careful and not overstep. So he urged the Wittenbergers to be true in their love for each other and be careful that not to become "noisy gongs or a clanging cymbal" as the Apostle Paul cautioned.[30]

These sermons and Luther's presence largely calmed the uproar and after his return, the community settled back into a new routine.[31] They now established a "new normal" for their lives together. However, many questions remained for the community. A question of great importance was concern that now that they were separated from Rome, who would educate their clergy? How was parish discipline to be applied?

In 1526–28 the need for visitations to parishes became apparent. As a result, in 1528, Luther acquiesced to Phillip of Hesse's desire to have local officials visit congregations. Initially he was wary of this as he did not want it to be seen as governmental control over church issues. However, out of concern for the parishes and also the compensation of priests in these communities, he agreed.

---

28. Luther, *Theological Writings*, 289–90.
29. Ibid., 292.
30. Ibid., 304.
31. Bainton, *Here I Stand*, 272; Lohrmann, *Book of Harmony*, 37–38; Nestingen, *Martin Luther*, 57–58. A dramatic exception to this relative peace was the "Peasants' War" in 1525. Peasants, emboldened by new ideas and facing economic challenges due to changes in the feudal society revolted. Luther was sympathetic to the peasants, but when they revolted, he rejected this breach of temporal authority and wrote harshly against them. The brutality of the lords in crushing the revolt, in part justifying themselves with Luther's words, lost him the support of the peasants and was a blot on his career—one of many times Luther spoke too quickly and too harshly.

Section 2: Assessing Martin Luther's Leadership

The Saxon visitations created another opportunity for Luther to engage his followers as well as see the troubling realities in parishes. While many priests were serving faithfully, there were those who were woefully uneducated and lacking in knowledge and experience. Additionally, the conditions and compensation for priests varied widely, and life without papal authority was changed.[32] Parish churches were being underserved and were under serving their clergy. A cycle of neglect had set in that had resulted in a general lack of education and knowledge.[33]

The Saxon visitations could not correct all of these issues. However, they did create awareness for Luther and the leaders of the Evangelical community as to the needs of the people for resources. The visitations exposed to Luther a general lack of knowledge or awareness of the lay community in the basics of the faith. Luther responded by providing resources for worship as well as instruction but also challenging the communities to take responsibility for their own needs and actions. He created an adaptive tenet, the "holding environment."[34] Ultimately, this need led him to the third and final example of this chapter, the writing of *The Small Catechism* beginning in 1528 and completing the work in 1529.

SMALL CATECHISM

For young people growing up in a Lutheran congregation, it is hard to overstate the importance and influence of Luther's Small Catechism. It's simple and forthright style, focusing on the basics of the faith, continue to make it relevant, and it has been translated into many languages. Even today, the catechism is often the central instructional tool for youth and young adult Christian education in Lutheran congregations around the world.

The Saxon Visitations had exposed the clear need for a catechism, or primer of the faith, with which families could teach their children. As a result, Luther set about in this time developing such a resource. The catechism focused in on teaching the basics of the faith: the Ten Commandments, Apostles' Creed, the Lord's Prayer, the Sacraments, and prayer. Each commandment or

---

32. Luther, *Theological Writings*, 324.

33. Ibid., 322. In his usual unshrinking tone Luther wrote about the visitations of the "deplorable, wretched deprivation" he had witnessed.

34. Bainton, *Here I Stand*, 319–20, 334; Nestingen, *Martin Luther*, 72–75. Luther provided hymns, liturgies, and of course the translation of the Bible to the communities. His impact on the German language and culture as a result was immense and continues to this day.

section of the creed or prayer was broken down and Luther asked a simple question, "Was ist das (What is This)?"[35]

Today most learners encounter the catechism as a small book or pamphlet. However, in Luther's time, they were printed up poster sized to be hung in kitchens or living rooms. Parents were expected and instructed to then use this resource to teach their children these basics of the faith. In so doing, they also were reminded of the basics of their faith and also to encourage themselves and their children toward literacy in the German language.

Luther also saw the catechism as a tool for the church as a social organization. He was not unaware that there were many who did not share his faith or who had actively chosen to reject faith. He did not advocate forcing individuals to believe as he knew that faith was a gift of God. Yet he saw value in a shared sense of values within a community and that the commandments at least could provide this encouragement and shared sense of commonality.[36]

The Small Catechism was a revolutionary adaptive leadership tool. Recognizing the dislocation of society Luther did not attempt to simply recreate the educational institutions of the Roman church. Rather, Luther shifted the focus of faith formation from church to home. He admonished the people to learn the faith and respect the sacraments out of love for God and desire to receive God's mercy, not fear of authority. In so doing he weaved his theology of the cross into the entire document.[37]

The Small Catechism was another way Luther was continuing to build on his initial adaptive move changing the purpose of good works from pleasing God to a response to God's grace. It was one of the works he truly prized and prayed would continue to last long after his death.[38] Luther was both providing for followers but also giving the work back in order to encourage them to take responsibility for their faith development, not as a requirement for righteousness, but as a response to the gift of faith.

---

35. Kolb and Wengert, *Book of Concord*, 346; Lohrmann, *Book of Harmony*, 43–44.

36. Kolb and Wengert, *Book of Concord*, 345, 365; Luther, *Theological Writings*, 323–24. Despite many challenges and changes, Luther lived in a homogenous society. A postmodern worldview would reject this sort of assumption of a common metanarrative for a community. This is just one of the challenges of translating the work and example of Luther and other historical figures for contemporary leadership. However, one of the adaptive leader's challenges is to work with followers to find meaning and learn together what acceptable outcomes are considered positive for the community.

37. Lohrmann, *Book of Harmony*, 54–56; Luther, *Theological Writings*, 325.

38. Bainton, *Here I Stand*, 348.

Section 2: Assessing Martin Luther's Leadership

CONCLUSION

Combining modern leadership theory with historic examples of leadership opens up new understanding, insight, and appreciation for the work of those who have led in the past. The current chapter has demonstrated how Martin Luther worked as a leader in ways that today would be understood as adaptive leadership. In particular, he demonstrated through his actions many of the keys of adaptive leadership theory as defined by Ronald Heifetz. Table 3 gives a summary of these keys and examples of Luther's adaptive work.

Table 3. Examples of Luther's Adaptive Leadership

Adaptive Leadership Trait	Examples
Identify the Adaptive Challenge	-95 *Theses* -Exposed Indulgence Abuses -Theological Shift (Two Kinds of Righteousness)
Keep Level of Distress in a Tolerable Range (Create a Holding Environment)	-Theology of the Cross -Saxon Visitations -Sermons and Teaching at Wittenberg
Focus Attention on Ripening Issues Not on Stress Reducing Distractions	-95 *Theses* -Heidelberg Disputation -*Small Catechism*, addressing lack of education in churches and with clergy.
Give Work Back to the People	-Freedom of a Christian (Call to Servanthood) -Saxon Visitations -*Small Catechism* -Translation of the Bible (giving the Word of God to the people)
Protect Voices Without Authority	-95 *Theses* and writings against Indulgences -Sermons at Wittenberg (protecting laity from his own followers)

From this table it is clear that Luther worked in ways that connect with adaptive theory. Luther's example encourages leaders to be honest and recognize changing paradigms of authority and culture. Yet while recognizing these changing worldviews, Luther reminds leaders of the vital importance of standing firm in their own convictions despite the challenges of threats the leader might face.

Finally, and most importantly, this chapter has demonstrated Luther's keen focus on assuring and caring for his followers. His study of Scripture and pastoral heart for those living in fear of damnation drove his theological breakthrough. He desired throughout his life to ensure the lay people of Germany were not abused or taken advantage of either by the followers of the pope or his own followers. In so doing, he demonstrated that more modern concepts emphasizing the importance of followers to leaders have deep roots in the past.

Luther made a great many errors throughout his life, as do all leaders. However, this study helps to both better understand Luther's actions and their impacts on followers. Additionally, by observing Luther's leadership, future leaders are guided in how they might respond to the challenges of changing institutions and worldviews. Luther's time, although separated from today by five hundred years, was not all that different than the twenty-first-century world. The clash of civilizations, worldviews, rising nationalism, and focus on the individual resonates today as it did in the early sixteenth century. In theology and in leadership, Luther continues to remain as relevant today as he was five hundred years ago.

7

Luther as a Transformational Leader

Dr. Jay Harley

There is no doubt the Reformation radically transformed the Christian church. This movement began when a little known monk and theology professor named Martin Luther attached his list of 95 *Theses* to the door of the Palace Church in Wittenberg. Beginning as a list for theological and academic discussion and debate, these ninety-five theses launched a movement that transformed the course of human history. This chapter will explore Luther as a transformational leader focusing on his leadership from the posting of the 95 *Theses* through reforming and organizing a Protestant church.

Martin Luther is certainly an appropriate subject to examine as a transformational leader. Even though the theory of transformational leadership was not initially popularized until 1978 by James McGregor Burns, Luther and the movement surrounding him exemplify many of the qualities of transformational leadership as described by modern leadership scholars. The movement was strikingly transformational with results lasting hundreds of years and continuing today.

The movement of reformation cannot be attributed to Luther alone, as other aspects of culture, government, religion, and even technology served as significant catalysts for the Reformation. For example, the copying of the original 95 *Theses* and other later Luther writings using the printing press definitely spread Luther's message rapidly and heightened the transformative effects of his work. The German citizens' displeasure with the pope and the

Church made Luther's writings trendy and also created a willingness among the people to distribute and at times even read aloud his work to the masses.

While it is too simplistic to think that Luther accomplished the Reformation alone with only his leadership and knowledge, Luther as an individual was a transformational leader. Even with other people and elements aiding his cause, Luther was the definitive leader and pioneer of a Reformation of the Christian church. It was Luther's thoughts and convictions which prompted the writing of the theses and later works. It was Luther who had to defend himself and his beliefs before nobility, priests, diets, and councils. It was Luther who boldly preached and spoke publicly against the egregious practice of indulgences. It was Luther who influenced students and worked tirelessly to translate the New Testament into German so that more people would have access to the written word of God. It was Luther who risked his life for his convictions and the true message of the gospel—justification by faith alone. Luther's personal leadership was certainly transformational. He led from his passion for truth, led publicly, and led on a personal level as he engaged with people about issues of theology and Christian practice.

This chapter will analyze Luther as a transformational leader and evaluate his actions and behaviors in light of transformational leadership theory. Also, this chapter will analyze the state of the church during Luther's day and contrast Luther's transformational leadership to the decidedly transactional theology of the Roman Catholic Church.

TRANSFORMATIONAL LEADERSHIP THEORY

According to Gill, transformational leadership and its contrasting view, transactional leadership, are the most discussed and prominent leadership theories of modern leadership scholarship.[1] In the late 1970s, James Macgregor Burns's 1978 classic on leadership brought the idea of transforming leadership to the forefront of contemporary leadership discussion and scholarship.[2] For Burns, a transforming (now commonly referred to as transformational) leader has the interests and benefits of followers in mind while leading and focuses on the needs and collective interests of followers. This was the major principle for Burns's understanding of leadership: the leader acts to better the situation for followers.[3] A transformational leader not only focused on results that were advantageous for followers but, as Ronald Heifetz commented, "should elevate

---

1. Gill, *Theory and Practice*, 82.
2. Burns, *Leadership*.
3. Ibid., 3.

Section 2: Assessing Martin Luther's Leadership

followers to a higher moral level."[4] Heifetz considered this higher moral level as feeling affection, connection to community, common benefit, and service. The transformational leader envisions followers' lives being enriched along with accomplishing goals. According to Northouse, transformational leaders, "provide followers with a vision and sense of mission."[5] Followers often admire the transformational leader because of the leadership behaviors exhibited by the transformational leader.[6]

Transformational leadership was identified to be closely connected to the servant leadership theory, and many similarities exist between the two understandings of leadership. Both servant leadership and transformational leadership have a unique interest in the needs and improvement of followers over the needs and wants of the leader.[7] The following chapter, however, will look at how servant leaders, especially biblical servant leaders, follow the guidance of Scripture and the direction of the Holy Spirit in determining the needs of others.

Burns did not envision a selfish leader who wields power and influence for personal benefit; he envisioned a true leader as someone who considered the needs and purposes for the collective group and not just the leader. Therefore, a ruthless dictator who lives in wealth while his constituents live in poverty would not be considered a transformational leader. The ruthless dictator is not utilizing power to benefit followers but instead is focused on making his own life more comfortable. Later leadership scholars began referring to this type of leadership as pseudo-transformational leadership.[8] This type of leadership may appear effective and produce some type of results, but it does not accomplish the goals of followers. A true transformational leader will lead with a collective interest in mind.

Burns expressed his understanding of leadership, and his comments provide a helpful summary of the thinking behind his development of transformational leadership theory:

> Some define leadership as leaders making followers do what followers would not otherwise do, or as leaders making followers do what the leaders want them to do; I define leadership as leaders inducing followers to act for certain goals that represent the values

---

4. Heifetz, *Leadership without Easy Answers*, 21.
5. Northouse, *Leadership*, 182.
6. Ibid., 180.
7. Gill, *Theory and Practice*, 90.
8. Bass and Riggio, *Transformational Leadership*.

and the motivations—the wants and needs, the aspirations and expectations—of both leaders and followers.[9]

Burns conceived of leadership in a way that involved both the process of leadership and the results of leadership. The ends and the means of leadership were connected, and the results did not justify the way the leader led. Leaders often focus on positive results, but for transformational leadership, the results were not the only or even the most important factor in leadership. The way the leader led was of great importance to Burns and his advancement of the idea of the transforming leader. A transformational leader must actively lead as a transformational leader, not just obtain positive or lasting results.

Burns recognized transformational leadership as the highest form of leadership, and while he certainly acknowledged the existence and, at times, necessity of transactional leadership, he believed transformational leadership should be the goal of every leader. Burns defined leadership comprehensively as:

> The reciprocal process of mobilizing, by persons with certain motives and values, various economic, political, and other resources, in a context of competition and conflict, in order to realize goals independently or mutually held by both leaders and followers.[10]

In this definition, leadership is identified as a mutual gathering of leaders and followers, where the leader may not always be the individual who initiates the mobilization of an interested group to accomplish a task. Also, the leader is not alone in accomplishing a purpose and is not the only gifted individual involved. Burns believed leaders and followers bring multiple resources to the mission. Since the leader and the followers contribute valuable resources to the mission, the leader realizes the value of the giftedness of the followers and involves them in the leadership process. Burns also fittingly saw that transformational leadership occurred "in a context of competition and conflict."[11] Therefore, the climate around the leaders and followers may not be supportive of their purpose. The leadership activity may be difficult, and within the difficult surroundings, the transformational leader endeavors to accomplish goals and solve problems important to the leader and to followers.

Luther's leadership behaviors and attitude certainly correlate to Burns's comprehensive definition of leadership. Luther engaged and organized others in the leadership process in an environment that was hostile to his viewpoints.

---

9. Burns, *Leadership*, 19.
10. Ibid., 425.
11. Ibid.

Section 2: Assessing Martin Luther's Leadership

Luther also demonstrated profound care for his followers, the common people of Germany. Burns discussed the idea of the intellectual leader and confirmed the place of a leader that led with ideas. The communication of innovative and radical ideas was considered a possible component of transforming leadership.[12]

Luther also was reinforced and encouraged by others around him. Hendrix affirmed that the support of Luther's other academic colleagues aided him even before the publishing of the 95 Theses as he formed his trademark theological ideals.[13] The resources of others furthered Luther's causes considerably with the accessibility of printing documents and books as a major catalyst of Luther's notoriety which provided him a platform for influence. Hendrix also discussed the impact of the printing of Luther's works as the multiple printings and distribution of the 95 Theses spread Luther's viewpoints dramatically.[14] Luther's influence increased rapidly as his intellectual and theological ideas spread as his written works were published and distributed.

Luther maintained significant interest in what was best for his followers and not for him personally. He believed passionately that the eternal destiny of the souls of his followers was at stake and took personal risks in order to do what was best for the people of Germany. He spoke boldly against the religious establishment in order to improve the standing of the common people. For example, Luther is quoted as saying, "All I wish to do is to arouse and set to thinking those who have the ability and the inclination to help the German nation become once more free and Christian, after the wretched, heathenish and unchristian rule of the pope."[15] As seen in a few examples, Luther's leadership aligned with Burns's explanation of the transforming leader. Later in this chapter, Luther's leadership will be analyzed in light of Kouzes and Posner's model of transformational leadership.[16]

Transformational Leadership Contrasted with Transactional Leadership

Burns championed the place and role of the transformational leader, but he also acknowledged the existence and place of transactional leadership. Since Burns's definitions of transformational leadership were provided in this

---

12. Burns, *Leadership*, 144.
13. Hendrix, *Martin Luther*, 68.
14. Ibid., 62.
15. Luther, *Address to the Christian Nobility*, 74.
16. Kouzes and Posner, *Leadership Challenge*.

chapter, his definition of transactional leadership is also important to understand as the two theories of leadership will be contrasted. Burns defined transactional leadership as follows: "Such leadership occurs when one person takes the initiative in making contact with others for purpose of an exchanged of valued things."[17] Transactional leaders according to Gill are "strongly directive and they tend not to use the consultative, participative or delegative styles."[18] Transactional leadership focuses upon contingent rewards to followers. The followers are rewarded in certain ways based upon performance and the meeting of goals set by the leader. As Burns identified transformational leadership as having a focus on the means of the leadership process and the attention of the leader on the development of the followers, transactional leadership, in contrast, devotes emphasis on the results from the transaction from the leader to the follower. However, in this description, transactional leadership provides greater clarity in outcomes of the leadership process than transformational leadership.

Luther as a Transactional Leader

Attempting to describe Luther as a transactional leader would be difficult as a foundational aspect of transactional leadership is the leader having some type of power over the followers. Luther had a position of authority as a professor, but as he led a movement of reform, he did not have significant authority to give rewards or offer negative feedback in which he could force followers to change behavior. A major component of Luther's leadership of the Reformation was the fact that he led without a position of authority. He led much of the movement with the religious authorities of his day in opposition to him. Burns identified this reality of leadership by declaring, "All leaders are actual or potential power holders, but not all power holders are leaders."[19] Luther mostly led without the power to initiate transactions with followers and led without official authority.

TRANSFORMATIONAL LEADERSHIP CONNECTED TO CHARISMATIC LEADERSHIP

While transformational leadership focused on the mutual purposes between leader and followers along with the development of the followers through the

17. Burns, *Leadership*, 19.
18. Gill, *Theory and Practice*, 83.
19. Burns, *Leadership*, 18.

Section 2: Assessing Martin Luther's Leadership

leadership process, charismatic leadership focused on the personality of the leader. According to Northouse charismatic leadership is often closely connected to transformational leadership and sometimes even used synonymously.[20] Charismatic leaders can influence followers through their personalities and act in certain ways that have influence on their followers. Charismatic leaders are deemed to have compelling personalities and an established set of core beliefs.[21]

Luther as a Charismatic Leader

When discussing Luther as a transformational leader, evaluating his leadership in relation to charismatic leadership is essential. Without authority or given power to lead with transactions, Luther's personal charisma was a key factor in his leadership effectiveness. Luther's personal charisma was recognized during his own lifetime and during the time of the Reformation. In the formative biography of Luther, *Here I Stand*, Bainton described the view of Luther's personality:

> In the early years of the Reform a cartoon appeared portraying Luther as "the German Hercules." The pope is suspended in derision from his nose. Beneath his hand cowers the inquisitor Hochstraten, and about him sprawl the scholastic theologians. The caption reveals that Luther had become a national figure.[22]

Bainton also examined how Luther's writings contributed to the growth of his charismatic personality. The wide distribution of Luther's writings was previously discussed in this chapter and is mentioned here again to emphasize the importance of this factor in the growth of Luther's leadership. The spread of Luther's writings caused Luther to become well known in Germany and in other countries as well. Luther received letters informing him that his teaching was being spread secretly in Rome.[23] Bainton summarized the popularity of Luther during this time, "Such acclaim made Luther the head of a movement which has come be known as the Reformation."[24] Luther's personality and charisma brought about by his boldness in teaching, speeches, and debates with the distribution of his writings fueled his influence as reform progressed.

---

20. Northouse, *Leadership*, 177.
21. Ibid.
22. Bainton, *Here I Stand*, 111.
23. Ibid., 113.
24. Ibid.

THE PERSONAL QUALITIES OF THE TRANSFORMATIONAL LEADER

As charismatic leadership intersects with transformational leadership, the personal qualities of a leader are important to effectiveness. The transformational leader must be personally trusted by followers in order to unify followers to accomplish a purpose. Gill commented on the importance of the personality of the transformational leader, "Such leaders also gain the admiration, respect, trust and confidence of others by personally demonstrating extraordinary abilities of one kind or another. They put the needs of other people before their own, and they display high standards of ethical and moral behavior."[25] The personal qualities of the leader are directly connected to the leadership behaviors of the transformational leader.

For transformational leadership to occur, the leader's personal qualities would be key to acceptance and trust from followers. In a practical sense, this would mean that the leader procures trust from followers by demonstrating his/her care for followers. The transformational leader establishes and communicates a vision and purpose in which the followers feel needed. The followers of a transformational leader believe that the leader and the joint purpose is what is best for all involved. Luther naturally embodied personal qualities which endeared him to the people of Germany throughout the Reformation. The people perceived Luther as a leader fighting for their best personal, economic, and spiritual interests. Luther communicated the vision intellectually while also communicating the vision in ways for the common person to grasp and support.

This steady support from the people of Germany was influenced by personal decisions Luther made. These personal decisions increased his impact among the people and led to greater leadership effectiveness. Luther believed strongly in the importance of bringing the pastor's message to the common people in a way that they could understand. Thus, he argued that the sermon should be delivered in German, that the congregation should sing in German, and that hymn writers develop songs that could teach congregants about the basics of faith. This was a significant change initiated by Luther as the worship service in Wittenberg was previously conducted in Latin, meaning most of the people attending the service would not have understood. The goal for Luther was to bring his message to the common people. His purpose was a deeply spiritual purpose as he was not trying to expand his own personal brand or increase his own fame, but believed that the people needed the truth of the gospel in order to move from spiritual darkness to salvation.

25. Gill, *Theory and Practice*, 84.

Section 2: Assessing Martin Luther's Leadership

The attention to the personal qualities of the transformational leader also leads to the major criticisms of transformational leadership theory. Rather than transformational leadership occurring as leadership behaviors, the criticisms state that transformational leadership regards leadership as a trait or attribute of the leader. Therefore, a leader could not learn to be a transformational leader. Northouse described this criticism of transformational leadership, "There is also a tendency to see transformational leaders as people who have special qualities that transform others. These images accentuate a trait characterization of transformational leadership."[26] In the original description of transformational leadership by Burns, he presumed that individuals could learn transformational leadership.[27]

TRANSFORMING FOLLOWERS

Transformational leaders should have an intentional focus on the development of followers. Throughout descriptions of transformational leadership, the attention to the improvement and growth of followers is described as one of the paramount features of transformational leadership in practice. Burns described this facet of transformational leadership as the leader appealing to the "hearts and minds" of followers and guiding them to move to higher motives and understanding of purpose.[28] Burns also emphasized that the transformational leader marshals followers to fresh thinking and organized action.[29] The transformational leader should produce followers who continue the purpose and lead after the transformational leader is no longer leading. Twentieth-century German Lutheran theologian Dietrich Bonhoeffer knew of the impact of Luther's followers, "Luther had said that grace alone can save; his followers took up his doctrine and repeated it word for word."[30] For Luther, the movement continued with great momentum after his death. Followers were motivated, transformed, and compelled to continued action after Luther.

Through his writing, speaking, and teaching, the results of Luther's leadership inaugurated a Reformation of the Christian Church and altered the religious and cultural landscape of Europe. The effects of Luther's work continue five hundred years after the 95 *Theses* were first introduced as suggestions for debate. The lasting results of Luther's leadership were due to the

---

26. Northouse, *Leadership*, 193.
27. Burns, *Leadership*.
28. Ibid., 459.
29. Ibid., 429.
30. Bonhoeffer, *Cost of Discipleship*, 49.

spiritual connection of his message to the people of his day. Marty examines the impact of Luther, "Why this wide effect and appeal? Luther would have answered: because the heart of his theology and practice reached the human heart at its deepest fonts."[31] The followers transformed by the message of Luther continue his work, and his theological and spiritual contribution endures.

It is too narrow of a view to only recognize Luther's impact on the theological thought and practice of the Christian Church. Luther grasped the correlation of all aspects of life and culture to faith. Marty also discussed the importance of the influence of Luther in other areas than just theology or the church:

> Secular commentators in Luther-anniversary years often make much of Luther's contribution to the spread of human liberty beyond the world of church and spirituality. The cultural contributions after October 31, 1517, are also vast. Thus it happens that Luther himself had a passionate interest in music, and encouraged the participation of musicians in both the church and outside of it. People in his tradition also had great impact on law.[32]

As Luther began his resistance and disconnected from the established Catholic Church, he was able to impact other arenas where the church did not control. Through these broader areas of influence and interest, he was able to extend the spread of his message of reform. Through his lasting impact in all of these various areas of faith and culture, Luther demonstrated the marks of a transformational leader. His followers continued the movement and the broad results of the movement continue today. By understanding transformational leadership theory and its application to Luther, he can be appreciated as a transformational leader.

LUTHER AS A TRANSFORMATIONAL LEADER

As transformational leadership theory and practice was described, the connection to Luther's leadership was drawn and some examples of Luther's leadership were described in order to demonstrate Luther's transformational leadership. Luther remains one of the most important figures in the history of the Christian Church, and many accounts of his writing and leadership exist that can illustrate his leadership practices.

---

31. Marty, *October 31, 1517*, 86.
32. Ibid., 85.

Section 2: Assessing Martin Luther's Leadership

Kouzes and Posner formulated a model of transformational leadership to categorize practices of transformational leaders.[33] The Kouzes and Posner model described five broad categories of transformational leadership behaviors. The five categories of transformational leadership behavior from Kouzes and Posner are:

1. Model the Way
2. Inspire a Shared Vision
3. Challenge the Process
4. Enable Others to Act
5. Encourage the Heart

Stories, quotes, and accounts from Luther's life will be connected to these five categories to represent his transformational leadership behaviors. The Kouzes and Posner model provides an organized way to present these leadership behaviors. Due to the large amounts of material on Luther, not every account and aspect of Luther as a transformational leader can be included in this chapter. The purpose of connecting some of his leadership behaviors to the Kouzes and Posner model is to provide the reader with an overview of how he led to begin and carry out the reformation as a transformational leader.

Model the Way

To model the way, a transformational leader, effectively communicates values and vision to followers while setting an example and building trust with followers.[34] Luther modeled the way through his own wrestling with matters of faith. He was known as a consistent confessor of his own sins while a monk.[35] He did not accept authority because it was the authority but critically thought about matters of the Bible and faith. As Luther struggled with the message of Romans, he had his own reformation experience of faith which then led him to begin teaching followers about the new idea of justification by faith.[36] Luther explained his new understanding of faith in *A Treatise on Christian Liberty*:

---

33. Kouzes and Posner, *Leadership Challenge*.
34. Northouse, *Leadership*, 188.
35. Hendrix, *Martin Luther*, 41.
36. Ibid., 52.

> But this faith cannot at all exist in connection with works, that is to say, if you at the same time claim to be justified by works, whatever their character; for that would be to halt between two sides, to worship Baal and to kiss the hand, which, as Job says, is a very great iniquity. Therefore the moment you begin to believe, you learn that all things in you are altogether blameworthy, sinful and damnable, as Romans 3:23 says, "For all have sinned and lack the glory of God;" and again, "There is none just, there is none that doeth good, all have turned out of the way: they are become unprofitable together." When you have learned this, you will know that you need Christ, Who suffered and rose again for you, that, believing in Him, you may through this faith become a new man, in that all your sins are forgiven, and you are justified by the merits of another, namely, of Christ alone.[37]

As seen from Luther's own words, he communicated his belief on faith in Christ, a belief that was in direct conflict with the established Catholic Church.

Luther also modeled the way as he faced opposition from the religious and political establishment on his views of theology. His personal safety was threatened, and he abandoned many personal comforts and benefits by espousing ideas that were in direct conflict with the Catholic Church. As Luther stood in opposition to the Catholic Church, the idea of justification by faith was not the issue which caused him the most trouble. The logical product of justification by faith alone was the fact that justification through any works was invalid and not a true gospel. Therefore, the visits to relics and the payment of indulgences did not justify someone before God, and in Luther's opinion made people further from God. As Luther spoke against customary practices of the Catholic Church which brought the church income and cemented allegiance among the people, he was vehemently opposed even by the pope himself.

Inspire a Shared Vision

The second transformational leadership practice by Kouzes and Posner focuses upon the leader's engagement of followers to embrace and participate in carrying out a collective purpose.[38] Luther was able to communicate the belief of justification by faith and speak in opposition to the Catholic Church's practices of indulgences and other works-based approaches to salvation and righteousness. Luther did this through multiple methods. He taught in the

37. *LW* 31:227.
38. Kouzes and Posner, *Leadership Challenge*.

Section 2: Assessing Martin Luther's Leadership

academic classroom, he preached boldly, he wrote profusely, and he led the now famous Table Talk discussions in his home. As stated earlier in this chapter, the ability for Luther's writings to be printed and distributed to the general population boosted the spread of his message and vision. The easier practice of printing even allowed Luther to publish his translation of Scripture and allow it to be in the hands of the common people. His writing is known to have inspired other Reformers from nearby countries who read his writing and were motivated to lead as well. Through each of his activities communicating his beliefs, he was sharing a vision of spiritual truth and inspired others to embrace the truth while halting participation in the purchasing of indulgences.

Challenge the Process

The third component of the model of transformational leadership may be the aspect of leadership in which Luther is best known. Luther definitively challenged the status quo and the momentous system of the Catholic Church, and he did so at the enjoyment of the German people. In his younger years, Luther did not directly attempt to split from the pope. He did speak against aspects of papal authority and beliefs. As summarized by Hendrix, "Although Luther's reproaches of the papacy became harsher with age, in his early years evidence suggests he questioned papal authority in mainly three matters: the scam of indulgences, the absence of pastoral concern in the Roman hierarchy, and the lack of historical and biblical evidence for papal supremacy."[39] In his younger years, other Reformers considered Luther not radical enough and distanced from him.[40]

At times in his life, he sarcastically offended religious and political leaders and demonstrated to others that the norms of the day could be challenged. Luther preached in Wittenberg telling of his opposition to the theological beliefs of the Catholic Church during his day. Luther is speaking against a decree by the pope:

> Against such fools' laws we have preached, and set forth that no sin is involved in these foolish prescriptions of the pope:, and that a layman does not commit sin if he touch the cup or the body of Christ with his hands. You should give thanks to God that you have: come to such clear knowledge, which many great men have lacked.[41]

39. Hendrix, *Martin Luther*, 16.
40. Ibid., 156.
41. Haemig, "Invocavit Sermons," 34.

Luther was challenging justification through works, and in this instance, he was stating that following the pope's edicts did not bring right standing with God. Luther challenged the status and the norms and boldly communicated this to all who listened. Challenging the Catholic Church did bring results to the reform movement as the desire for reform spread and in certain parts of Germany the purchasing of indulgences was ceased, clergy were allowed to marry, and the importance of relics was diminished.[42]

Enable Others to Act and Encourage the Heart

The final two aspects of the model of transformational leadership were closely connected in Luther's leadership practices. Luther was consistently enabling other people to take action as part of reform through his writing and speaking. He desired for others to take up the mantle of opposition to the pope and in favor of reformation. The Kouzes and Posner model of transformational leadership described encouraging the heart as the capability of the transformational leader to reward followers for their investment in the shared purpose while nurturing and inspiring followers to future action.[43]

Luther created the environment of the Reformation which allowed others to take action against the papal authorities and for correct theological teaching. In 1522, Luther wrote directly against insurrection or armed resistance, so he did not advocate physical violence as action to bring further reformation.[44] By communicating his sermons and his writings in German, he was able to convey his message to the common people which certainly inspired them to join the movement of resistance to the Church.

Luther wrote *For All Christians, Warning Them against Insurrection and Rebellion* in 1522, and this important work is outlined as a guide for how to act appropriately as a Christian in bringing reform to the Church. Luther began his message with the strong biblical truth that God will bring judgment to the pope and the Catholic Church for its misleading teaching and abuses. Luther encouraged the heart by reminding his followers that even when difficulty and opposition from Church and government authorities existed, they could trust in God's judgment on their opponents. Luther assured his followers that they were on the correct side of the understanding of the gospel.

Along with the reassurance of God's coming judgment on the Church and its allies, Luther provided his followers with three points of action. First,

---

42. Hendrix, *Martin Luther*, 156.
43. Kouzes and Posner, *Leadership Challenge*; Northouse, *Leadership*, 188.
44. Hillerbrand, "Christian Life," 281.

Section 2: Assessing Martin Luther's Leadership

Luther instructed his followers to confess their own sin in order to recognize their own shortcomings to lead to repentance. Luther warned his followers to do this in order to check their own motives. Second, Luther direct them to pray against the pope and his system of authority. Finally, Luther challenged them to speak out directly against the papal authority and in favor of the true gospel of Jesus Christ. Through this final action, Luther wanted the message to spread and expose the deceit of the Church alongside the truth of the Bible. The warning and instructions given by Luther in *For All Christians, Warning Them against Insurrection and Rebellion* was clear coaching from Luther to his followers on how to expand and preserve the movement. Luther was the clear and definitive leader, but he appreciated the opportunity for others to act and spread the message.

The teaching, speaking, writing, and action of Luther created an environment where others were encouraged to take action and continue this movement even after his death. Luther's writings were utilized as the primary instruction standard for the earliest Protestant churches. Theological debate and other reforms continued after Luther's death which exemplifies the transformational leadership of Luther. He created an environment where, as he led, he enabled others to act and lead.

Long before transformational leadership theory was ever discussed and popularized, Luther led with qualities of a transformational leader. He led in a way that inspired his followers, changed the faith system of his day, and allowed for others to continue the movement. His leadership produced conditions that compelled others to continue reformation and for this movement to be discussed five hundred years after it began.

THE TRANSACTIONAL RELIGION OF LUTHER'S DAY

Magnifying Luther's transformational leadership practices was the transactional religious practices of the sixteenth century. When Luther drafted the 95 *Theses*, all aspects of the Christian faith presented to the German people were individual or a series of transactions to make a person right with God. The Catholic Church built the entire Christian faith around these transactions and failure to participate in these transactions alienated a person from the church and society. Sproul wrote of Luther's goal related to these transactions of religion, "One of the deepest ongoing concerns Luther had as a pastor was to liberate his congregation from the chains of superstition."[45] The rote religious transactions lacked feeling and authenticity for the common person, and they

---

45. Sproul, *Legacy of Luther*, 281.

felt obligated to participate to remain in good standing with the Church or to experience some other type of spiritual benefit from participation. The common people were unable to read the Bible in their own language, so they would have had no way to dispute these transactional practices. Many of the administrators of these transactions took advantage of the opportunity to increase their own personal wealth.

The most well-known religious transactions of Luther's day were the visit to relics and indulgences. An understanding of these two religious transactions aids in the understanding of Luther's message and also demonstrates the contrast between Luther and the belief and practice of the Catholic Church. This stark contrast amplified Luther's leadership distinctiveness and effectiveness as a spiritual leader in the sixteenth century. Luther was delivering a different message than the church leaders. He was presenting a view of God and faith that did not cost exorbitant amounts of money. He proclaimed clearly the message of justification by faith and not justification by works.

Indulgences

Indulgences were ways by which an individual could obtain full or partial pardon from sin allowing the person to avoid time in purgatory. Luther spoke directly against indulgences especially the sale of indulgences. The *95 Theses* devote significant time to indulgences. For example, thesis 21, "Therefore those preachers of indulgences are in error who say that, by the indulgences of the Pope, a person is made exempt and saved from all punishment."[46] The indulgences captured the indignation of Luther even more as they were sold to individuals.

The practice of the sales of indulgences began during the time of Pope Leo X, and the funds were used to build St. Peter's Basilica in Rome. Leo X brokered a deal with Albert of Brandenburg in Germany for the sale of indulgences whereby Albert would gain the most influential Church position in Germany and one-half of the profits of the sale of the indulgences. The other half of the profits from the sale of these indulgences would be sent to Rome and used for the construction of St. Peter's Basilica. John Tetzel was the lead salesman of indulgences in Germany and traveled preaching this message. Gonzalez documented Tetzel's message:

> Tetzel and his preachers were heard announcing that the indulgences that they sold made the sinner "cleaner than when coming out of baptism," and "cleaner than Adam before the Fall," and

46. Marty, *October 31, 1517*, 99.

that "the cross of the seller of indulgences has as much power as the cross of Christ." Those who wished to buy an indulgence for a loved one who was deceased were promised that, "as soon as the coin in the coffer rings, the soul from purgatory springs."[47]

Tetzel's passionate preaching and marketing was one of the main factors compelling Luther to begin speaking more publically against the corruption of the Church. Luther even wrote directly against this specific practice in thesis 28, "It is certain that when money clinks in the chest, avarice and greed may increase, but the intercession of the Church depends on the will of God alone."[48] He also included condemnation for the sale of indulgences in thesis 35:

> People do not preach any kind of Christian doctrine who teach that sorrow for sin and repentance are not necessary for those who buy souls out of purgatory or buy letters of indulgence.[49]

Luther's disapproval for the sale of indulgences was one of the main places of disagreement with the Catholic Church's teaching and practice. He considered the sale of indulgences as incorrect theology and taking advantage of the people of Germany.

With the awareness of the sale of indulgences on the mind of people throughout Germany, Luther proclaimed a different message. The sale of indulgences was a transaction that gave people pardon from God's punishment. Luther's communication to the people was not a message of transaction but a transformational message. For example, thesis 68 considered the purchase of indulgences incomparable with the true grace through Jesus, "Yet they are in reality in no way to be compared to the grace of God and the devotion of the cross."[50] Luther not only spoke against the indulgences but in favor of the gospel which was not focused on fleecing the people of their money and teaching the people incorrect theology. Luther spoke, taught, wrote, and worked to give the people full access to the knowledge and truth of God. He opposed the transaction to give the people access to the transformational gospel.

Relics

The other significant religious transaction of Luther's day was the visit to relics. Like indulgences, visiting a certain relic would relieve the individual, a

---

47. Gonzalez, *Story of Christianity*, 21.
48. Marty, *October 31, 1517*, 100.
49. Ibid., 101.
50. Ibid., 107.

relative, or someone else identified by the individual from some aspect of the judgment of God such as reduction of the sentence to purgatory. The Catholic Church claimed the allotting of spiritual benefits from the saints with visiting associated relics, and often the primary benefit was the reduction of time in Purgatory.[51] Luther had interest in religious relics, and in 1510, he even traveled all the way to Rome in order to visit many important relics. Luther's visit to Rome was not for leisure or sightseeing, but he intended his visit to reap the spiritual benefits of Rome, especially the opportunity to revere as many religious relics as possible.[52]

Luther's doubt of the efficacy of relics began while in Rome. He witnessed the insecurity and blatant debauchery of religious leaders in Rome, and even while exercising his duty at the site of the relics began to become disheartened. Luther did not leave Rome with a sense of spiritual renewal; instead, he departed disappointed and doubtful. It was not until around seven years later that the *95 Theses* were circulated, but the questioning of the transactional religion he experienced had commenced.

> Preaching his final sermon, Luther discussed relics: "After all, there is preaching every day, often many times every day, so that we grow weary of it. . . . Alright, go ahead, dear brother, if you don't want God to speak to you every day at home in your parish church, then be wise and look for something else: in Trier is our Lord God's coat, in Aachen are Joseph's pants and our blessed Lady's chemise, go there and squander your money, buy indulgences and the pope's secondhand junk."[53]

Luther characterized the visit to relics similarly as the purchase of indulgences. The relic system was an established transaction that distracted from the true gospel and supposedly offered people an authentic connection with a spiritual benefit from some item or individual from the Bible or the history of Christianity.

In this religious climate, people treated faith, the church, and God as a series of transactions, and the more transactions completed, the more benefits received. The system of religion was callous and consistently fleeced common people of their meager means. The system and its leaders did not appear to care for the people of Germany and seemed to only desire them to participate in more religious transactions which cost more money. In the midst of this system was Martin Luther. It was because of this system that

---

51. Bainton, *Here I Stand*, 32.
52. Ibid., 34.
53. Sproul, *Legacy of Luther*, 281.

Section 2: Assessing Martin Luther's Leadership

Luther was compelled to take action and speak against this system. Others in Germany felt that Tetzel and his allies were presenting false doctrine, and they only quietly voiced their concerns.[54] Luther, though, declared his opposition boldly, and his message was entirely contradictory to the primary message of the Church. Luther was not asking for the people to participate in purchasing more indulgences or visit more relics, but he was advancing a message of justification by faith alone.

The transactional religious system of his day magnified Luther's transformational leadership practices. Luther as the transformational leader was pointedly distinct from the other religious leaders of the sixteenth century. As other leaders advocated and forced a transactional religious system, Luther's stood out. The glaring contrasts between Luther and the Church religious leaders amplified Luther's work and message. The contrasts may have produced an environment which led to greater success for the movement of reform by Luther.

CONCLUSION

Northouse summarized the activities of a transformational leader and stated that transformational leaders energize followers, become examples that followers can imitate, have confidence, communicate strongly, elicit trust from followers, and cast a clear vision.[55] Luther exemplified transformational leadership practices and began and led a movement of reform that had lasting results. Luther cared for the common people of Germany and led differently than the religious leaders of his day. He remained committed to the vision in spite of substantial opposition and conflict. Luther's leadership commitment came from a deep spiritual belief and desire to ensure that this correct truth was taught and available to all of the people of Germany. Hundreds of years before transformational leadership theory was popularized, Martin Luther led the Reformation as a transformational leader.

---

54. Gonzalez, *Story of Christianity*, 22.
55. Northouse, *Leadership*, 190.

8

Luther's Pastoral Leadership

Mark A. Cook

INTRODUCTION

Eugene Peterson, in his book *Working the Angles*, minces no words about the plight of being a pastor in contemporary times:

> I don't know of any other profession in which it is quite as easy to fake it as in ours. By adopting a reverential demeanor, cultivating a stained-glass voice, slipping occasional words like "eschatology" into conversation and heilsgeschichte into our discourse—not often enough actually to confuse people but enough to keep them aware that our habitual train of thought is a cut above the pew level—we are trusted, without any questions asked, as stewards of the mysteries.[1]

The propensity for pastors to be identified by their outward posture, their "reverential demeanor," and the vocabulary they use reveals the confusing state of being a pastor in the twenty-first century. Barna's recent *The State of Pastors 2017* paints a vivid portrait of the myriad of pressures that crowd into pastor's lives: they are lonely, prone to self-doubt, feel increasing pressure to be popular

---

1. Peterson, *Working the Angles*, 6.

Section 2: Assessing Martin Luther's Leadership

rather than prophetic, and struggle with life-balance.[2] On top of existential concerns that beset contemporary pastors, there is also the struggle to try to fit into an unrealistic mold of what it means to be a "successful pastor." With the rise of mega-churches after World War II has come an increasing desire among parishioners for pastors to be charismatic, dynamic, smooth-talking, and attractive. Alongside these outward qualities, pastors are expected to be good at counseling, managing, leading, planning, budgeting, and mediating conflicts. This cavalcade of expectations causes many young pastors to try to focus only on what they are best at, in the vein of *StrengthsFinder*, putting people around them that have complementary giftings.[3]

How are pastoral leaders to respond to these increasing demands? I believe that pastoral leaders, who I will refer to in this chapter as anyone involved in full-time ministry, can gain greatest clarity by looking back. Eugene Peterson, in another book on pastoral ministry, *Five Smooth Stones for Pastoral Work*, argues that "there are no lines of progress in pastoral work along which later generations reach new levels, outdistancing and outmoding their predecessors . . . pastoral work operates out of a long tradition."[4] There is a wealth of wisdom and insight into pastoral work that can be found by exploring the lives of the great pastors of history. That is at the core of what this chapter aims to do through the magisterial figure of Martin Luther.

THE WORLD OF MARTIN LUTHER

Luther's vision for pastoral leadership is centered on the idea of service. Jesus' Great Commandment, recorded in the Synoptic Gospels (Luke 10:25–28; Mark 12:28–34; Matt 19:19) is a combination of two key texts in the Old Testament Pentateuch (Deut 6:5, "Love the Lord your God with all your heart and with all your soul and with all your strength," and Lev 19:18, "Love your neighbor as yourself"). The Johannine Gospel includes the seminal story of Jesus washing his disciples' feet, then declaring, "A new commandment I give to you, that you love one another: just as I have loved you, you also are to love one another."[5] These texts are at the heart of the Christian idea of servant leadership, and have shaped the way contemporary scholars have articulated the distinctive way Christians are to be different in leadership than their non-Christian counterparts. While Luther was of course not a student

---

2. Barna Group, "State of Pastors."
3. Rath, *StrengthsFinder 2.0*.
4. Peterson, *Five Smooth Stones*, 6.
5. John 13:34.

of leadership in the way contemporary scholars have been, using theoretical social-scientific lenses to analyze the subject, he *was* a student of Scripture. His vision for pastoral leadership was shaped by his immersion in it.

The great Reformation principle of *ad fontes* (going back "to the sources") birthed a renewal movement of reading Scripture.[6] Championed by Luther and others, this idea of going back and reading the foundational texts (not only for religious purposes, but also for law, philosophy, and other subjects as well) was unique because up until this point, reading the Bible was the privilege of the clergy alone. Erasmus's translation of the original Greek New Testament (*Novum Instrumentum*) in 1516 sent shockwaves throughout Europe, as Luther and others encountered texts like Matthew 4:17 in the original language rather their stilted Latin versions. Suddenly, texts like this, which had been rendered "do penance" in Jerome's Latin Vulgate, had their original meaning restored (in this case, "repent!" rather than "do penance").

Alongside the flourishing of new translations of the Bible by Erasmus, John Wycliffe, Miles Coverdale, and William Tyndale, the invention of the printing press by Johannes Gutenberg was the key technological innovation that breathed life into the *ad fontes* idea. Now, books went from being only accessible to those of great means or great education, to broadly available to a much larger swath of the population. So at the same time as Luther was discovering the truth and beauty of Scriptures for himself, he was able to encourage those who would come after him largely because the printing press made Scripture accessible on a larger scale.

For Luther, *ad fontes* went well beyond reading Scripture; it comprised an entire way of thinking about life, and, more specifically, pastoral leadership. If it is true that we need to go back "to the sources" continually, then pastoral leadership needs to be concerned with the origins of calling and the fountainhead of service to others. Luther was fundamentally concerned with what it meant to be a pastor, which led him to devote much of his extensive writing on the subject to the matters of pastoral calling and pastoral service. What does it mean to be called by God, and what then does a pastor do to serve God and others? Luther wrestled with these questions through the lens of the Great Commandment's call to love and serve God and others, arriving at a vision for pastoral leadership that emphasized true calling and true service.

---

6. For in-depth treatment of this point, see George, "*Ad Fontes!*"

Section 2: Assessing Martin Luther's Leadership

THE PASTOR'S CALL: PASTORS NEED TO BE CALLED BY GOD

Luther's theology works itself out into all facets of his beliefs, including his vision for pastoral leadership. This volume includes a brief review of the central tenets of Luther's theology, but the three most important theological ideas for this chapter's purposes are justification by faith (*sola fide*), theology of the cross (*theologia crucis*), and the primacy of Scripture (*sola Scriptura*). Luther was a master dialectical theologian, using the power of contrast to highlight important themes, as Timothy George notes:

> He spoke almost invariably in sets of twos: law and gospel, wrath and grace, faith and works, flesh and spirit, with respect to God or the world (*coram Deo/coram mundo*), freedom and bondage, God hidden and God revealed.... Truth can only be arrived at by way of confrontation with a contrasting truth.[7]

Max Depree, a contemporary leadership scholar, defined the first and most important task of the leader is to "define reality."[8] Luther's ability to cut to the core of the matter, defining the stark differences between his views and those he wished to dismantle, allowed him to be a natural thought leader for what would be known as the Reformation. His clear articulation of theology, through a variety of styles of polemical writing, only further helped him become a beacon for other Reformers to follow. His *95 Theses* and *Heidelberg Disputation* are examples of simple logical arguments. *The Bondage of the Will* exemplifies his ability to draw out counterarguments and refute them. His various pastoral letters to friends and clergy showcase his ability to incisively offer guidance and counsel while also exhibiting care and concern. He modeled the tenets of leadership that Bill George thought were most important: a leader must understand their purpose and have a strong set of guiding values.[9] He also had the ability to articulate his vision to others, which is a key facet of leadership nearly universally affirmed by contemporary leadership scholars. Whereas in contemporary culture this manifests itself in the need for leaders to be persuasive speakers and proficient verbal communicators, Luther's great skill was in how he could articulate his vision through writing. He was certainly no second-rate orator, but his vision spread primarily as a result of his writings.

---

7. George, *Theology of the Reformers*, 61.
8. Depree, *Leadership Is an Art*, 11.
9. George and Sims, *True North*.

The foundation of Luther's theological framework rested on the pillar principle of justification by faith. Set forth clearly in the Smalcald Articles of 1538, justification by faith is:

> The first and chief article: That Jesus Christ, our God and Lord, "died for our trespasses and was raised for our justification" (Rom. 4:25); and he alone is "the Lamb of God, who bears the sin of the world" (John 1:29); . . . Now because this must be believed and may not be obtained or grasped otherwise with any work, law, or merit, it is clear and certain that such faith alone justifies us.[10]

Dietrich Bonhoeffer describes this as, "We *become* the righteousness of God. In Christ's death God's righteousness triumphs for our benefit."[11]

Luther believed this was the most important component of theology. For him it was not only a theological concept but something that impacted all of one's life, as Kurt Hendel describes:

> Luther's consistent emphasis on justification by grace through faith throughout his writings reflects his reading of Paul. It is also informed by his spiritual quest for a gracious God. The radical good news that faith alone justifies embodied the gospel for Luther and brought peace and comfort to his troubled soul, particularly during his persistent *Anfechtungen*, or spiritual struggles. The doctrine of justification was never simply a theological construct for the reformer. It was God's ultimate message of grace addressed to all of humanity. It is for this reason that Luther insisted that on "this article stands all that we teach and practice."[12]

From a letter to George Spenlein we can grasp more clearly how deeply this idea penetrates the heart and soul of the Christian: "Learn Christ and him crucified. Learn to praise him and, despairing of yourself, say, 'Lord Jesus, you are my righteousness, just as I am your sin. You have taken upon yourself what is mine and have given to me what is yours. You have taken upon yourself what you were not and have given to me what I was not.'"[13]

This fundamental theological principle translated into how Luther conceived of pastoral leadership and is mirrored in the way he articulated a pastor's call. Luther distinguished between two different types of call: the inner call (God speaking to the individual) and the outer call (God speaking to the

---

10. Hendel, "Smalcald Articles," 429.
11. Bonhoeffer, *Theological Education*, 354.
12. Hendel, "Smalcald Articles," 429.
13. Maxfield, "Selected Letters," 434.

Section 2: Assessing Martin Luther's Leadership

individual through the community of faith).[14] The importance of calling was not merely for the edification of the church, it was also to help the pastor when doubt and despair crept in: "Therefore, we who are in the ministry of the word have this comfort, that we have a heavenly and holy office; being legitimately called to do this, to prevail over all the gates of Hell. On the other hand, it is dreadful when the conscience says: 'You have done this without a calling!'"[15] Justification by faith is not only a doctrine that speaks to the truth about our status before God, but is also a truth to carry in your heart when temptation and despair come your way. In similar fashion, Luther's belief that calling must come from God also not only speaks to the status of a pastor's position before their congregation, but also helps the pastor when they are confused and weary.

Leadership as a contemporary field of study is constantly undercut by popular-level best-selling books that offer lists of hackneyed platitudes, empty of any particularity, but promising rewards of success to those who will spend the money on the book. This genre of leadership often emphasizes what people need to *do* to become better leaders. Leadership that begins with the *what* rather than the *who* is doomed from the start. Even more, the pastor who does not understand their call is in a precarious position.

Many contemporary Christian leadership writers affirm what Luther established through his articulation of the importance of calling. Blackaby and Blackaby's *Spiritual Leadership* argues that a Christian leader is concerned with moving people on to God's agenda. In their conception, leadership is more than an occupation, which means that "calling comes *before* vocation."[16] Christian leaders, and especially pastors, need to examine *who* they are in Christ, and *how* they are called, before they figure out *what* they need to be doing. Henry Nouwen takes a similar approach in his work *In the Name of Jesus*. He decries leadership that is based on power games, insisting that Christian leaders must lead from their relationship with Jesus. This means that they have to constantly return back to the source of their call, rather than simply trying to improve themselves through external adjustments. Blanchard and Hodges popular *Lead Like Jesus* offers a four-way understanding of Christian leadership, with one being the heart of a leader. Within the heart, the leader constantly needs to be asking questions about their motives and their attunement to God.

For Luther the importance of a pastor's calling is primary because they must see themselves as servants of God in all things:

---

14. For in-depth treatment of this point, see Wilson, "Luther on Preaching."
15. *LW* 40:62.
16. Blackaby and Blackaby, *Spiritual Leadership*, 127.

> At this point, you may ask, "If all people in the church are priests, by what name do we distinguish those we now call priests from the laity?" I respond that an injustice has been done to these words—"priest," "cleric," "a spiritual one," and "a churchman"—when they are transferred from all other Christians to those few who now are called by this faulty usage "churchmen." For Holy Scripture does not distinguish at all among them, except that it calls "ministers," "servants" and "stewards" those who now are proudly labeled popes, bishops, and lords but who should be serving others with the ministry of the word in order to teach the faith of Christ and the freedom of the faithful. For, although it is true that we are all equally priests, nevertheless we cannot all serve and teach nor, even if we can, ought we all to do so publicly. As Paul states in 1 Corinthians 4:1: "Let a person regard us as servants of Christ and dispensers of God's mysteries."[17]

The pastor who understands that they must serve God rather than themselves returns frequently to the origin of their call. Luther's argument is a rebuke to contemporary ministry culture that has little space or time for deep reflection. The call stories of Abraham (Genesis 12), Moses (Exodus 3), Samuel (1 Samuel 3), Isaiah (Isaiah 6), Ezekiel (2), and others in the Bible provide rich biblical examples of the pattern for how God calls those he wants to use for specific purposes. One of the central concerns of Luther was to emphasize how God's call focuses on the willingness and obedience of the person called rather than the external labels and rewards of the labor. In his day, the Catholic Church's leadership had become infested with men who were only seeking power, wealth, and influence. After deep immersion in the Scriptures, though, Luther saw a pattern that did not meet with his culture's view of calling. He therefore sought to reestablish the importance of ministers and pastors seeing themselves as servants of Christ and their neighbor rather than servants of their own self-interest.

Luther's theology of justification by faith was not the only part of his theology that impacted the way he envisioned pastoral calling. His theology of the cross (*theologia crucis*) also gave greater shape to how he understood the importance of a pastor's call. The central place where he articulated his theology of the cross was in the Heidelberg Disputation. Within this powerful set of theses, Luther systematically contrasts the difference between the theologian of glory with the theologian of the cross.

---

17. Wengert, "Freedom of a Christian," 507.

Section 2: Assessing Martin Luther's Leadership

> (19) "That person does not deserve to be called a theologian who looks upon the invisible things of God as though they were clearly perceptible in those things which have actually happened."
>
> (20) "He deserves to be called a theologian, however, who comprehends the visible and manifest things of God seen through suffering and the cross."
>
> (21) "A theologian of glory calls evil good and good evil. A theologian of the cross calls the thing what it actually is."[18]

Luther draws such a sharp contrast between the two ways because of how corrupt the Catholic Church's leadership had become. During his time, Church leaders had tremendous wealth, status, and security. The pastoral vocation had become too comfortable, with ministers enjoying great material affluence. Luther's study of Scripture pushed him to question the lavish lifestyles he witnessed in Church leaders, eventually leading him to label the two ways as the way of glory versus the way of the cross. The theological derivation of this idea had reverberations throughout other parts of Luther's thought, including how he envisioned the pastor examining the cost of the call before accepting the call. Paul Althaus summarizes the difference between Luther's two pathways of theology:

> The theology of glory seeks to know God directly in his obviously divine power, wisdom, and glory; whereas the theology of the cross paradoxically recognizes him precisely where he has hidden himself, in his sufferings and in all that which the theology of glory considers to be weakness and foolishness. The theology of glory leads man to stand before God and strike a bargain on the basis of his ethical achievement in fulfilling the law, whereas the theology of the cross views man as one who has been called to suffer.[19]

To best understand how the theology of the cross works itself out in the particularities of a pastor's calling several threads have to be connected. The best way to approach this is to juxtapose Luther's vision of calling with how it challenges contemporary Christian notions of calling.

Faithfulness over Success

Today in America, many pastors jump into the ministry vocation based on visions of success rather than visions of faithfully serving the Lord. This

---

18. Luther, *Theological Writings*, 15.
19. Althaus, *Theology*, 27.

phenomenon is similar to what Luther encountered in many of the religious leaders of his day. Success replaces faithfulness when outward appearances including financial and material growth become more important than the inward condition of the heart.

Blackaby and Blackaby discuss the pernicious impact this orientation has on how the minister leads:

> Some leaders set the goals for their organization based on what will bring them the most personal success or praise.... Religious leaders may lead their churches to build larger auditoriums or to televise their services, not because they genuinely sense God's leadership to do these things but in order to enhance their reputation as preachers. Such egocentric leadership is generally cloaked in statements of loyalty to the organization or in pious proclamations about the kingdom of God. But in truth, the growth of the organization merely feeds the leader's pride.[20]

Augustine argues in *City of God* that the first sin of our parents (Adam and Eve) was the sin of pride, or willfully desiring independence from God.[21] C. S. Lewis builds on Augustine's argument by summarizing how human pride comes down to a basic decision humans make every day: "There are only two kinds of people in the end: those who say to God, 'Thy will be done,' and those to whom God says, in the end, '*Thy* will be done.'"[22] Pride is the chief enemy that Luther fights against when he describes the pastoral vocation because it so dramatically challenges the call of God.

The American obsession with success that many pastors carry with them can be attributed to the larger program of self-fulfillment that has been at the heart of twentieth-century cultural thought. Kenneth Gergen's book *The Saturated Self* describes how Americans moved from community-oriented to self-oriented, substituting community goals like the common good for selfish goals like personal material acquisition. With success as the goal, pastors become enslaved to results. It is easy to conceal selfish success in hollow spirituality by merely adopting a vocabulary that communicates how success brings glory to God. The problem, however, is that success is never the goal of Christian ministry in the Bible. Luther's emphasis on a pastor seeing their call as a call to service is founded in this principle. Dietrich Bonhoeffer, a Lutheran pastor in Germany during the rise and rule of Hitler, describes how success

---

20. Blackaby and Blackaby, *Spiritual Leadership*, 60.
21. Augustine, *City of God*, bk. 14, ch. 13.
22. Lewis, *Great Divorce*, 75.

Section 2: Assessing Martin Luther's Leadership

causes people to shift from thinking about the way something is done to only caring about the results:

> Where the figure of a successful person becomes especially prominent, the majority fall into *idolizing success*. They become blind to right and wrong, truth and lie, decency and malice. They see only the deed, the success. Ethical and intellectual capacity for judgment grow dull before the sheen of success and before the desire somehow to share in it. People even fail to perceive that guilt is scarred over in success, because guilt is no longer recognized as such. Success per se is the good.[23]

When material success is the underlying reason a pastor goes into ministry, they essentially limit how God can use and shape their ministry. The call narratives of the Old and New Testaments emphasize faithfulness rather than success, and Luther's grounding in Scripture allowed him to see how important this part of calling is for pastors. If they start from a place of wanting success, they miss the fruit of service through faithfulness to God. To use Dallas Willard's phrase, they must "abandon outcomes to God," learning to see that the world is ordered by God's appointments, not by human achievements.[24]

Weakness over Strength

One of the most popular recent books on leadership is *StrengthsFinder*. Its argument is that leaders need to focus on discovering their areas of strength and then work to maximize those areas rather than trying to improve in their areas of weakness. While the book has a useful role in helping clarify dimensions of a person's giftings, Luther would be strongly opposed to adopting it wholeheartedly as an avenue for pastors to explore their call. Yet, it has become a leading book in shaping the way many pastors think about their vocation. If someone is naturally gifted at preaching, this model would argue that they need to let other people on staff do the bulk of the administrative and pastoral care duties. In essence, the philosophy behind *StrengthsFinder* is built on the idea of specialization.

The problem, though, is that the Bible seems to offer a more nuanced understanding of weakness and strength. Paul's letters to the Corinthians offers the Pauline vision for how weakness can ultimately give more glory to God. In 1 Corinthians 1:18, he starts by declaring that: "The word of the cross is folly to those who are perishing, but to us who are being saved it is the power of

---

23. Bonhoeffer, *Ethics*, 89.
24. Willard, *Renovation*, 209.

God." He continues several verses later, arguing that: "But God chose what is foolish in the world to shame the wise; God chose what is weak in the world to shame the strong." After setting up the paradoxical nature of weakness and strength in the kingdom of God, he moves in his second letter to show how this idea of human weakness gives glory to God: "But we have this treasure in jars of clay, to show that the surpassing power belongs to God and not to us." Finally, as he closes his letter, he culminates his argument about weakness being an avenue to bring glory to God by applying it to his own deep struggles:

> But he said to me, "My grace is sufficient for you, for my power is made perfect in weakness." Therefore I will boast all the more gladly of my weaknesses, so that the power of Christ may rest upon me. For the sake of Christ, then, I am content with weaknesses, insults, hardships, persecutions, and calamities. For when I am weak, then I am strong.

That last phrase is the capstone of Paul's theology of weakness, and it is what also undergirds Luther's understanding of the pastoral vocation. Luther's theology of the cross, seen specifically in the twentieth thesis in the *Heidelberg Disputation*, argues that true Christians see God through his suffering on the cross in Jesus. Having faith in God is an ultimate leap that shows weakness by the world's standards, yet that is exactly how Luther believes pastors should be oriented toward God. In his work *On Christian Freedom*, he summarizes his point: "Still, because faith alone suffices for salvation, I do not need anything else except for faith exercising its power and sovereignty of freedom in these things. Look here! This is the immeasurable power and freedom of Christians."[25] J. I. Packer builds on Luther's work about the power of weakness in the pastoral vocation in his work *Weakness Is the Way*. In this short book, Packer describes how our weaknesses give glory to God because they drive us to look more deeply for Christ, love him more completely, and lean on him in greater dependence:

> When the world tells us, as it does, that everyone has a right to a life that is easy, comfortable, and relatively pain-free, a life that enables us to discover, display, and deploy all the strengths that are latent within us, the world twists the truth right out of shape. That was not the quality of life to which Christ's calling led him, nor was it Paul's calling, nor is it what we are called to in the twenty-first century. For all Christians, the likelihood is rather that as our discipleship continues, God will make us increasingly weakness-conscious and pain-aware, so that we may learn with Paul that

---

25. Wengert, "Freedom of a Christian," 505.

Section 2: Assessing Martin Luther's Leadership

when we are conscious of being weak, then—and only then—may we become truly strong in the Lord.[26]

THE PASTOR'S TASK: REMAIN FAITHFUL TO THE WORD

So far in this brief exploration of Luther's vision for pastoral leadership, we have argued that Luther's theology of justification by faith and his theology of the cross undergird his understanding of the importance of the pastor's call. Now we move to the pastor's task. How does pastoral faithfulness work itself out in the daily and weekly tasks of a pastor? This is the kind of question that many of Luther's best writings wrestle with. He was an eminently practical, boots-on-the-ground person, applying his theology into every part of daily living. While justification by faith and the theology of the cross are fundamental to understanding his idea of pastoral calling, the central theological concept that sheds light on his understanding of the pastoral responsibilities is *sola Scriptura*. The idea of *sola Scriptura* is part of the larger "solas" of the entire Reformation, as John Frame summarizes: "by grace alone (*sola gratia*), by faith alone (*sola fide*), through Christ alone (*solo Christo*), on the basis of Scripture alone (*sola Scriptura*), to the glory of God alone (*soli Deo gloria*)."[27] In essence, as Paul Althaus and others have shown in their studies on Luther's theology, all of Luther's thought rests on this epistemological foundation. If *sola Scriptura* is true, then naturally one will look to Scripture as the primary substantiating fountain for the rest of theology. So Luther's justification by faith and theology of the cross naturally owe their origin to the epistemological idea of *sola Scriptura*. Justification by faith is the launchpad of Luther's theology, but the foundation that the launchpad is built upon is *sola Scriptura*.

Sola Scriptura in Preaching

Hughes Oliphant Old posits that Scripture alone has authority in the church, and that Christ is present to the congregation specifically through the preaching of that Scripture:

> Luther's theology of the Word is the bedrock on which his preaching was based. In fact, that was the secret of its effectiveness. For Luther, to preach was to preach the Word of God, and that meant nothing less than to teach the Scriptures and exhort the

---

26. Packer, *Weakness*, 53–54.
27. Frame, *History*, 169.

congregation to live by them. . . . Preaching is a matter of reading the Bible, explaining its meaning for the life of the congregation, and urging God's people to live by God's Word.[28]

Luther disdained how so many of the bishops in the Catholic Church had abdicated the role of teaching and preaching the Scriptures. In the preface to his *Shorter Catechism*, Luther bemoans this lack of responsibility:

> The deplorable, wretched deprivation that I recently encountered while I was a visitor has constrained and compelled me to prepare this catechism, or Christian instruction, in such a brief, plain, and simple version. Dear God have mercy, what misery I beheld! The ordinary person, especially in the villages, knows absolutely nothing about the Christian teaching, and unfortunately many pastors are completely unskilled and incompetent teachers. Yet supposedly they all bear the name Christian, are baptized, and receive the holy sacrament, even though they do not know the Lord's Prayer, the Creed, or the Ten Commandments! As a result they live like simple cattle or irrational pigs and, despite the fact that the gospel has returned, have masterfully learned how to misuse all their freedom. O you bishops! How are you ever going to answer to Christ, now that you have so shamefully neglected the people and have not exercised your office for even a single second? May you escape punishment for this! You forbid the cup [to the laity in the Lord's Supper] and insist on observance of your human laws, while never even bothering to ask whether the people know the Lord's Prayer, the Creed, the Ten Commandments, or a single passage from God's Word. Woe to you forever![29]

His answer to the lack of instruction in Scripture was to offer catechisms that ordinary people could use in their daily lives to ground themselves in the basic truths of Scripture. The best leaders do not merely criticize the problems they observe around them, but seek to actively offer solutions to the problems. Luther's solution to the problem of lack of instruction in the Scriptures was to encourage pastors to return to preaching directly from the Bible and to provide catechisms for congregations to use in daily life.

---

28. Old, "Age of the Reformation," 38.
29. Wengert, "Small Catechism," 212–13.

Section 2: Assessing Martin Luther's Leadership

Preaching to Felt Needs

One of the primary problems of contemporary American preaching is that it is oriented toward the felt needs of the individual rather than the edification and instruction in God's Word. This reductionist tendency is what manifests itself in a proclivity to preach primarily "how-to" sermons, or any number of well-intentioned topical sermons. Instead of beginning with the importance of instructing people in the Scriptures, contemporary pastors begin with the needs they perceive in their congregants. Eugene Peterson explains the subtle effect this has on preaching:

> What do people want from me, their pastor? Something surely along the order of a better life: encouragement, insight, consolation, formulas that enable them to get along better in a difficult world, that uplift them (a friend calls this "brassiere theology"). We, of course, are conditioned to comply. Why should we not please the people who pay our salaries if we can do it with good conscience? And why should not our consciences be good, ratified as they are by the vote of congregation after congregation? This consumerism shapes us without our knowing it. There is nothing in our lives that it does not touch in one way or another. This acquisitive mode is so culturally expected and congregationally rewarding that it cannot fail to affect our approach to the Scriptures. When we sit down to read the Scriptures we already have an end product in view: we want to find something useful for people's lives, to meet their expectations of us as pastors who deliver the goods.[30]

Preaching that begins with the needs of the individual will not truly meet the actual need, which is for edification in the Word. While this may sound as if it discourages against even mentioning real life situations people are struggling with, the opposite is true. The more a preacher grounds himself in the Scriptures, the more its natural perspicacity will emerge. It does not need to be made relevant to people's lives, because by its very nature Scripture is already the most relevant storehouse of truth.

Preachers that reduce their message to felt needs miss the opportunity to preach the entire counsel of Scripture. Hughes Oliphant Old explains how Luther believed strongly in preaching from a theological perspective that situated each individual passage within its larger biblical framework:

> Luther, as Augustine before him, had understood that there are in Scripture certain overarching themes in light of which the whole

---

30. Peterson, *Working the Angles*, 98.

of Scripture should be understood. The preacher should stress these themes, which should then lead him to put the passage before him into the perspective of the whole of Scripture.[31]

For Luther, the goal, or *telos* of preaching was never merely to instruct, but to lead people *through* instruction to Jesus: "Preaching, however, ought to serve this goal: that faith in Christ is promoted. Then he is not simply 'Christ' but 'Christ for you and me,' and what we say about him and call him affect us."[32] Herein lies the true leadership lesson for pastors seeking to learn from Luther: *The greatest act of service you can give your congregation is to regularly feed them with scriptural preaching that points ever and always to Jesus.* This core concept will shape and direct all the rest of the pastoral vocation. It requires pastors to immerse themselves more deeply in Scripture, but beyond that to learn how to pray and truly listen to what God is speaking through the Word.

CONCLUSION

Luther's vision for pastoral leadership is thus primarily concerned with becoming a servant leader. Through the power and purpose of the call all the way through to the completion of the task, pastors are to see themselves as servants of God rather than servants of their own desires. The theology of justification by faith provides pastors confidence that their call is not of their own doing. The theology of the cross encourages them to see their weakness as an opportunity for closer communion with God, as well as a way to give greater glory to God. The theology of *sola Scriptura* grounds the pastor in a concrete way of life centered upon the teaching and preaching of Scripture. Pastoral leaders can gain greater depth in understanding their call and task by studying Luther in more detail. Some of the greatest answers to the contemporary problems surrounding pastoral leadership in the twenty-first century can be found by looking back, *ad fontes* style, to the great stewards of the pastoral office in history, and few have left as deep an impression as Martin Luther.

---

31. Old, *Age of the Reformation*, 13.
32. Wengert, "Freedom of a Christian," 508.

9

Luther as a Servant Leader

Dr. Justin Gandy

INTRODUCTION

Thus far, Martin Luther has been labeled a change leader, an adaptive leader, a pastoral leader, a transformational leader, and now a servant leader. Certainly, he did not set out to be each of these kinds of leaders. So, which is he? Is he the über leader? Or, perhaps these leadership theories are not as unique as they purport.[1] Like many great leaders, Luther's life and leadership can be used to highlight numerous aspects of various leadership theories, and the same is true for servant leadership. Luther provides a superb example of an often overlooked aspect of servant leadership—determining what is in the best interest of followers.

Servant leadership was first introduced in an essay published in 1970 by Robert Greenleaf.[2] Some researchers, however, namely Sendjaya and Sarros,[3]

---

1. As a theory, servant leadership is often included as a subcategory of transformational leadership. Recently, servant leadership has been treated in the literature as a separate field of study (see Northouse, *Leadership Theory and Practice*). This chapter views servant leadership as distinct from transformational leadership specifically in terms of follower needs.
2. Greenleaf, *Servant as Leader*.
3. Sendjaya and Sarros, "Servant Leadership."

argue that servant leadership was first introduced to the world by Jesus when he taught his disciples they must first become servants if they wish to become leaders.[4] Nevertheless, servant leadership has continued to gain popularity in the leadership literature since its introduction in 1970 by Greenleaf. As the theory has matured, it has undergone subtle nuances in definition and expression.

One particular aspect of servant leadership is the focus on the interests of others, but very little has been done to explore who determines what those interests are or how they are developed. The biblical worldview offers a different understanding from that of Greenleaf regarding how leaders should determine what is in the best interests of their followers. In this aspect, Luther's life and theology provide a clear example. Luther was guided by his faith and by Scripture in determining what was in the best interest of his followers and thus became a true biblical servant leader.

The following sections will focus on servant leadership as a theory both from the classical perspective and from a biblical perspective. Special attention will be given to how each perspective understands and determines the needs and interests of others. Following that, a few of Luther's major decisions will be used to illustrate how he demonstrated true biblical servant leadership specifically in the area of serving follower's needs. This chapter will conclude with a brief discussion regarding implications for leaders today.

SERVANT LEADERSHIP

Classical

In 1970, Robert Greenleaf published *The Servant as Leader*, and it was updated and republished in 1991 and again in 2008. Greenleaf admits the words *servant* and *leader* are both overused, but he states, "I can find no others that carry as well the meaning I would like to convey."[5] It is important to note Greenleaf often prefers the phrase "servant and leader" as opposed to servant-leader or servant leadership. This is his way of helping the reader maintain an understanding of his belief that "the great leader is seen as servant first."[6]

---

4. See Mark 10:42–45.
5. Greenleaf, *Servant as Leader*, 7.
6. Ibid., 9.

Section 2: Assessing Martin Luther's Leadership

Definition

Greenleaf's revelation about servant leadership came as he was reading a short story by German author Herman Hesse, *Journey to the East*. The story is about a group of men who go on a pilgrimage to the east in search of ultimate truth. The central figure is Leo, a servant of the group who is happy and pleasant and who performs menial chores until he happens to disappear in a mountain gorge. The group falls into disarray, quarrels break out, and they disband the group and abandon the journey. Years later, one of the men finds Leo and discovers that he is in fact the great and noble leader of the order that sponsored the journey. The one who was known first as the servant was actually the leader, and Greenleaf believed the fact that Leo was known as a servant first was the key to his greatness as a leader. Leo was *always* the leader on the trip, but he was known first as a servant because that was his nature; it was who he was deep down inside. Greenleaf says of Leo, "Leadership was bestowed upon a man who was by nature a servant."[7]

Greenleaf believed the best leaders are those who by nature are servants. He uses language like "if one is a servant," "true servants," and "the natural feeling that one wants to serve."[8] This servant first leader then goes out ahead of others to show them the way. The leader does this through the adoption and implementation of several key behaviors including listening, understanding, communicating, periodically withdrawing, accepting, empathizing, foreseeing the unknowable, perceiving, persuading, and conceptualizing. For Greenleaf, these are the actions of a leader, but they can only be effective when performed by the one who is first a servant. Greenleaf would likely say that Luther was one of these "natural servants."

Greenleaf has been widely praised for his approach to leadership, but it is not without its problems. Significantly, there is the question of how one becomes a servant and whether or not this "natural feeling" is an inherent trait or something that can be developed. Greenleaf basically avoids the question and fails to help the reader understand how one should become a "natural servant." To compound the problem, Greenleaf states there is no "dependable way" to discern a true servant leader from an imposter.[9] Thus, at best, we are left hoping there are enough true servant leaders distributed throughout the world and that they somehow find their way into leadership positions.

---

7. Ibid.
8. Ibid., 15.
9. Ibid., 44.

Interests of Others

One significant aspect of Greenleaf's servant leadership theory is the emphasis on the interests of others. While some researchers consider servant leadership to be equivalent with transformational leadership, there is a distinct difference, and it hinges on the development of followers. Transformational leadership demonstrates care and concern for followers, and it does so specifically through the behavior labeled "individualized consideration" which includes "providing support, encouragement, and coaching to followers."[10] This individualized consideration is meant to address followers' higher-order needs, but those needs are often reduced to generic needs such as support and encouragement. While the transformational leader desires to see his or her followers "transformed" into better versions of themselves, the underlying motivation is not altogether altruistic.

For servant leaders, however, the focus is primarily on what is best for the followers. "A servant leader must attend to the needs of followers and help them become healthier, wiser, and more willing to accept their responsibilities."[11] Greenleaf said care must be taken by the servant "first to make sure that other people's highest priority needs are being served."[12] It is for this reason that Greenleaf believes servant leadership is the best option for future leaders. He believes that more and more, followers will only freely respond to those leaders who are proven and trusted as servants—as leaders who care deeply about the needs of their followers. This begs the question, however, of how those "highest priority needs" should be determined. Should the leader, the follower, or someone else determine the greatest need? This is where the biblical understanding of servant leadership provides some clarity, especially for Christ followers; and this is where Luther's life provides significant instruction as we uncover his primary motivation for understanding the needs of his followers.

Biblical

The research aimed at a distinctly biblical understanding of servant leadership is relatively limited.[13] In the research that does exist, there is little consensus

---

10. Yukl, *Leadership in Organizations*, 262.
11. Ibid., 420.
12. Greenleaf, *Servant as Leader*, 15.
13. For a more complete discussion regarding a biblical understanding of leadership, see the volume edited by Bell, *Servants & Friends*. Also see Jones, "Theological Comparison."

Section 2: Assessing Martin Luther's Leadership

about what constitutes a specifically Christian view of servant leadership.[14] Some conclude that the classical, or Greenleafian view, of servant leadership and the biblical view of servant leadership are essentially the same. Galen Jones, however, states, "A biblical perspective of servant leadership and a social science perspective of servant leadership do not share the same worldview. Although they have similar characteristics, for example, servanthood, others before self, and submission to authority; what makes them distinct are their religious and philosophical origins."[15] The Christian worldview presents a distinct and unique framework through which the ideas and applications of leadership must be viewed.

The Bible is not a text primarily about leadership, but it does contain much advice about leadership and examples of great leaders—especially Jesus. Paul's admonition of Jesus in Philippians provides the supreme example of biblical servant leadership. In Philippians 2:5, Paul instructs us to "have this attitude in yourselves which was also in Christ Jesus." What attitude is Paul referring to? He is referring to Jesus' attitude of service and how he focused on the interests of his followers.

Definition

Gene Wilkes published *Jesus on Leadership: Timeless Wisdom on Servant Leadership* in 1998 in which he defines a biblical servant leader as one who "serves the mission and leads by serving those who mission with him."[16] Wilkes highlights several characteristics of a servant leader including humility, followership, finding greatness in service, taking risks, taking up the towel, sharing responsibility and authority, and building a team.[17] Several of these characteristics are included in other leadership theories, but two are uniquely connected to servant leadership—finding greatness in service and taking up the towel.

A similar view on biblical servant leadership is presented by Don Howell when he states, "Biblical leadership is taking the initiative to influence people to grow in holiness and to passionately promote the extension of God's

---

14. Niewold, "Incarnational Leadership," argues that several non-biblical concepts from Greenleaf's original version of servant leadership have been adopted in Christian approaches but reflect a distorted view of Christ. He suggests serious theological work must be done in order to develop a proper Christian understanding of servant leadership.

15. Jones, "Theological Comparison," 122.

16. Wilkes, *Jesus on Leadership*, 18.

17. Ibid.

kingdom in the world."[18] Both Wilkes and Howell focus on the accomplishment of the mission, but they are quick to note that for the Christian, that mission should be wrapped up in God's mission and kingdom. A company may have its own mission statement, but a true biblical servant leader will ensure that mission coincides with and simultaneously advances God's mission. In other words, a biblical servant leader would never do anything that would harm or hinder God's redemptive work in the world including various elements of the company such as the mission itself, how employees, customers, and other stakeholders are treated, impact on the surrounding community, and all other business related decisions. A leader is a biblical servant when each of these areas is in alignment with kingdom principles.

One final definition will help round out our understanding of biblical servant leadership. Jim Plueddemann states, "Good leaders are fervent disciples of Jesus Christ, gifted by the Holy Spirit, with passion to bring glory to God. They use their gift of leadership by taking initiative to focus, harmonize, and enhance the gifts of others for the sake of developing people and cultivating the kingdom of God."[19] Note the similar focus on advancing God's kingdom as the ultimate objective of leadership, which is obviously something the classical approach to servant leadership does not include. Each of these definitions, however, does have something in common with Greenleaf's version of servant leadership in that all emphasize the interests of others.

Interests of Others

The biblical approach to servant leadership is not unique in focusing on the interests of others, but it is unique in the determination of those interests. Greenleaf advocates that leaders should help meet followers' highest priority needs, but he never defines what those needs might be. He does come close at one point by stating that leaders should help followers become wiser, healthier, and more willing to accept responsibility.[20] It is unclear, however, if Greenleaf believes wisdom, health, and responsibility are the "highest priority needs" of followers or if there are other needs that should be included. This is where the biblical worldview offers an advantage. In Matthew 6:8, Jesus assures us that God knows what we need before we even ask. As our creator and sustainer who knit us together in our mother's womb,[21] God knows us more intimately

18. Howell, *Servants of the Servant*, 3.
19. Plueddemann, *Leading Across Cultures*, 171.
20. Greenleaf, *Servant as Leader*.
21. See Ps 139:13.

Section 2: Assessing Martin Luther's Leadership

than anyone else, and it is he who knows what is in our best interest. This is a truth Luther knew well, and his insistence on *sola Scriptura* led him to use the Bible as his guide for determining the best interests of his followers.

This point is made clear in Wilkes's definition and his call for the servant leader to "take up the towel." With this statement, he is referencing the story of Jesus washing the disciples' feet in the upper room on the night he would be betrayed.[22] This story is often cited as an example for those who follow Christ to be servant leaders just like Jesus served. There is a life-sized statue of Jesus washing Peter's feet on the campus of DBU, and students are often reminded to be a servant as Jesus was a servant. The principle of the story, however, is not that we must wash other people's' feet, and those who reduce servant leadership down to physical acts of service have missed the point. This is where Greenleaf also seems to have gone astray. He was fascinated with Leo as a servant, and thus Greenleaf emphasized physical acts of service performed by the leader prior to any leading taking place.

There may be times when leaders are called to serve others physically, but the deeper principle is that leaders should do whatever is most needed in the moment. Wilkes further explains what he means by the behavior of taking up the towel. He says, "Dirty feet were not the real need. The disciples' discussion about greatness revealed their real need."[23] Wilkes rightly concludes that in that moment as the disciples were discussing who would be the greatest among them, their greatest need was to see their Lord and Master humble himself and perform a menial task. It was not about washing their feet; it was about doing something for them they desperately needed in that moment. It was about leading them by serving their needs. The question every biblical servant leader must ask is "What do my followers need most right now?" and the answer must not come from the follower nor the leader but from God who knows what each of us truly need.

The story of God leading the Israelites out of Egypt and through the wilderness provides a perfect example of biblical servant leadership. God led them by always doing for them what they needed most. Sometimes, he physically served them as he did when he brought them food or water.[24] At other times, God led them by giving them specific instructions on how to behave—most notably the Ten Commandments. There were times, however, when God led them through discipline. In Numbers 16, God is angry with Korah and his family, and he caused the ground to open and swallow the entire family and all their possessions. In that moment, God knew the people needed to under-

22. See John 13:1–17.
23. Wilkes, *Jesus on Leadership*, 157.
24. See Exod 16 and 17.

stand his righteous judgment.[25] God led them by serving them; by doing for them what was most needed. God has always done that, from covering Adam and Eve after their sin, to providing the Lamb to take away the sins of the world. God serves his followers' most important needs, but it does not always take the form of physical service like Greenleaf and others so often imply in servant leadership.

This emphasis on meeting follower's most important needs can also be seen in Howell's definition when he encourages leaders to help others grow in holiness. First Peter 1:16 states, "For it is written, be holy for I am holy." We become holy by becoming more like God, and becoming more like God is a process of refinement and growth in all areas of our lives. At times, we may need to be more like God in our confidence in boldness, and at other times, we may need to be humble and gentle. In the process of becoming holy, we will need different things at different times. A true biblical servant leader will help us meet those needs.

The key theological principle for understanding servant leadership is the concept of service. The biblical word most often translated servant is also sometimes translated as slave[26], and perhaps that imagery can help us understand what it means to serve. John MacArthur captures this well when he describes the life of a slave in the first century. He claims that the slave/master designation is the most commonly used description in the New Testament to describe followers of Christ, so it is appropriate to understand the role of a slave during the time of Christ. MacArthur states that many slaves functioned in various capacities—teachers, doctors, managers—depending on the needs of their masters.[27] Slaves meet the greatest needs of their masters. To be biblical servant leaders, we must meet the greatest needs of our followers.

Paul tells us to have the same attitude that Christ had when he decided to leave heaven and come to earth to offer himself as a sacrifice on our behalf. Paul writes in Philippians 2:4–7, "Do not merely look out for your own interests but also for the interests of others. Have the same attitude in you which was also in Christ Jesus who being in the form of God did not consider equality with God something to be grasped." Paul is reminding us that Jesus served us by doing what was in our best interest—namely that he leave heaven and come to earth—and we are supposed to behave in the same way.

---

25. In Exod 16:30, Moses tells the people that if Korah is swallowed up by the ground, then the people will understand that Korah and his family had spurned the Lord. Later, in vv. 38–40, Moses used Korah's censer as a sign and a reminder to the people to avoid the same mistakes.

26. δουλος—slave, servant, bondman; see ibid.; Mark 10:43–44.

27. MacArthur, *Slave*.

Section 2: Assessing Martin Luther's Leadership

God loves us, and he always does what is in our best interest, and thus, he is always a servant leader, even when his service to us comes in the form of punishment or rebuke. God is like any good parent who does what is in the best interest of the child even when it involves denying the child something he or she may desperately want. God directs, trains, corrects, rebukes, and does a myriad of other things for us, and all the while he is the supreme servant leader because he is doing for us what we need most in the moment. Jesus served his disciples; not just when he washed their feet, but at all times, and we are to have the same attitude. The difficulty comes in figuring out what is in the best interests of others. The following section will examine how Luther did what he thought was in the best interest of his followers and how his convictions led him to determine what those interests were.

LUTHER AS A SERVANT LEADER

The previous chapters in this book have outlined Luther's life and theology and many of the decisions he made as well as their impact on various aspects of the church and society. While there are several prominent examples of Luther serving the best interests of his followers, in this five hundredth anniversary year of his posting of the 95 *Theses*, perhaps it is appropriate to begin there.

As noted previously in the introduction to this book, Luther never intended the objections he posted on the door to be broadcast over all of Germany. He was responding to a specific situation and to specific teaching he believed to be false and harmful to the people. His primary concern was for the truth. At the top of the 95 *Theses*, he wrote, "Out of love for the truth and from desire to elucidate it, the Reverend Father Marin Luther . . . intends to defend the following statements."[28] Luther believed the people had long been duped by the papacy and the Catholic Church, and he was convinced that knowing the truth was in their best interest. Luther had already previously criticized the church's abuse of indulgences, and while he was grieved about the ones who were abused, he was convinced their greatest need was the truth, which would in turn prevent them from further abuse. Biblical servant leaders look beyond the immediate needs of the followers to those needs that are most pressing.

Luther continued his quest for the truth, and by so doing, he continued to do what was in the best interest of the people at the time. As he wrote essays that critiqued and opposed the orthodox positions of the Catholic Church, his following continued to grow. Luther did what he believed was in

---

28. Luther, *95 Theses*.

their best interest. He defended the truth against the tyranny of the Catholic Church, and he wrote treatises to the people to answer some of their practical questions.[29] He wrote against the vows of celibacy and was eventually married himself. He critiqued the practice of mass and called for its abolition because the people needed to understand that salvation was by grace alone and not by any work of merit.[30] Yet, at the same time, Luther believed that no one should be "dragged away from it by the hair"[31] because he knew the people needed to come to conclusions by their own conviction through faith alone and not through compulsion.

Some might argue that Luther's bitterness and relatively harsh treatment of the Jews provides an example quite the opposite of the servant leadership we are describing here. While his work *On the Jews and Their Lies*, in which he called the Jews "the devil's people," might seem severe and self-centered, Luther's motivation was for their greatest need as he saw it. He believed the Jews were blasphemers for rejecting the divinity of Christ and called for strict punishment against them "to see whether we might save at least a few from the glowing flames."[32] Perhaps he went too far in his resentment, but he truly believed punishment was in their best interest.

Another of his acts demonstrates his concern for the needs of the people but his reliance upon God to determine those needs. In 1522, Luther translated the Bible into the German language, which some consider to be his greatest achievement. "No other work has had as strong an impact on a nation's development and heritage as has this Book."[33] Luther wanted to strike a balance between a literal translation and a free interpretation because he knew the German people needed something that would speak to their hearts "as men do in the marketplace."[34]

Many of Luther's writings and actions have at their core a concern for the needs of others, but Luther made no pretense that he always knew what was best for others nor did he let his followers dictate their own needs. Luther was guided by his belief in Scripture alone and an unshakable commitment to certain theological principles as he determined what was in the best interests of the people. By being familiar with his followers, and guided by the convictions of Scripture, Luther accurately assessed and met the needs of his disciples and thus illustrates the essence of true biblical servant leadership. Servant leaders

29. Kittleston, "Early Years."
30. See Luther's Second Sermon, March 10, 1522.
31. *LW* 51:75.
32. Gritsch, *Martin Luther's Anti-Semitism*.
33. Zecher, "Bible Translation," 40.
34. Ibid., 41.

Section 2: Assessing Martin Luther's Leadership

put the needs of their followers first, and biblical servant leaders rely on Scripture and the guidance of the Holy Spirit in determining what those needs are.

Implications

Luther did not set out to become a servant leader. His desire was to serve God, and by doing so, he became a servant of others. He served the people by meeting their greatest needs at the time, and by doing so, he became their leader. Servant leaders today should emulate Luther as he followed Christ's example and Paul's admonition to put others' interests ahead of his own. Servant leaders do not merely look out for their own interest but also for the interests of others. The key difference, however, between classical servant leadership and biblical servant leadership is that biblical servant leaders allow Scripture to be their guide in determining the interests of others. In this, Luther provides a superb example.

Servant leaders must also keep in mind that serving someone does not automatically equate with physical service. Leaders serve their followers when they do what is best for them. Leaders can guide, instruct, coach, counsel, motivate, discipline, encourage, and perform a host of other behaviors all in the name of service when those behaviors are based on the wisdom of God about what is best for the follower. Leaders must not fall into the trap of believing they are only servant leaders when they are performing physical acts of service. If your boss never washes your feet, it doesn't necessarily mean he or she is not a servant leader. The true test is whether or not he or she does what is in the best interests of the followers.

CONCLUSION

Servant leadership has continued to gain popularity among both academicians and practitioners, but the focused has remained on serving the needs of others without much attention given to how those needs are determined. From a Christian perspective, servant leaders should focus on serving others by doing for them what it most needed in the moment. Much like a good parent sometimes says no and at other times says yes, a biblical servant leader is concerned about doing what is in the follower's best interest. Luther's life helps remind us that it is not enough to desire to serve others' interests, we must discern what those interests are, and they best way to do that is through reading the Bible and being guided by the Holy Spirit. In one of his sermons, Luther stated, "I simply taught, preached, and wrote God's Word; otherwise

I did nothing."[35] His focus was on obedience to God because he knew that following God would result in serving others in ways they needed most. As we contemplate Luther's life and example during this quincentennial year, may we serve and lead others the way Christ has served and led us.

---

35. *LW* 51:77.

Epilogue

Dr. David D. Cook

As we look back at the life of Martin Luther, we see that he had a great influence—not just on the people of his day, but on the contemporary Western world as well. He had a profound impact through his theology and also created waves that radically changed the makeup of many of our Western institutions. From the church, to politics, law, education, economics, and more, he left a footprint in society that can still be seen today.

But while these influences are certainly worthy of study, what this text has tried to do is analyze Luther as a leader who, though thrust into his position, had an immense impact on his followers. We have looked at him as a change agent, adaptive leader, transformational leader, pastoral leader, and servant leader. In these roles, we have noted that he influenced spheres as diverse as politics to church liturgy, theology to hymnody, and much in between.

In looking back at his leadership, the student of history can learn a great deal about how God can use even a humble monk to change the world. Just like many of the stories of leadership found in the Bible, Martin Luther's journey of leadership was winding and filled with ups and downs. He was certainly not perfect, and it was the acknowledgement of this imperfection that led him to rely on God's grace alone to make him righteous in God's sight. What we see from his life is that God can use a broken, sinful man who is nonetheless wholly devoted to seeking his call. And not only can God use such a man, but he can shake the very foundations of society.

While not all that Luther accomplished was positive (e.g., the ripple effects of his Reformation led to horrible wars and bloodshed for centuries to come), he nonetheless had a profound role in shaping the Western world in many ways that we take for granted today. But for all of his many areas of

Section 2: Assessing Martin Luther's Leadership

influence, I believe his key accomplishment was in drawing people back to the basics: the basics of God's Word and its implications for their lives. In compelling his followers to seek God's truth in its purest form, he set the stage for people to draw nearer to the God of all Creation.

As Christian leaders today, we, too, should make it our foremost goal to draw people closer to God and to illumine his truth in their lives. As Henry and Richard Blackaby shared in their book *Spiritual Leadership*, our primary goal must be to "move people on to God's agenda."[1] Instead of focusing on grand visions, opulent goals, and flashy milestones, our call is merely to help our followers keep their eyes on the One who can change their lives. As Os Guinness noted in his book *The Call*: "A life lived listening to the decisive call of God is a life lived before one audience that trumps all others—the Audience of One."[2]

Martin Luther did just that. In attempting to live his life before an Audience of One, he transformed the world of his day and left ripples that affect each of us today. While many authors may pontificate about his greatest legacy, it is my belief that his greatest mark as a leader was not in what he did, but in the One that he pointed others toward.

---

1. Blackaby and Blackaby, *Spiritual Leadership*.
2. Guinness, *The Call*, 70.

Bibliography

Althaus, Paul. *The Theology of Martin Luther*. Philadelphia: Fortress, 1966.
Augustine. *City of God*. Bk. 14, ch. 13. Edited by G. R. Evans. Translated by Henry Bettenson. New York: Penguin Classics: 2003.
Bainton, Roland H. *Here I Stand: A Life of Martin Luther*. Nashville: Abingdon, 1978.
———. "The Struggle for Religious Liberty." In *Church History* 10 (1941) 95–124.
Barna Group. "The State of Pastors." Video conference. 2017.
Bass, Bernard M. *The Bass Handbook of Leadership: Theory, Research, & Managerial Applications*. 4th ed. New York: Free Press, 2008.
Bass, Bernard, and Ronald Riggio. *Transformational Leadership*. Mahwah, NJ: Erlbaum, 2006.
Bebbington, David W. "The Evangelicals of the World." In *The Dominance of Evangelicalism: The Age of Spurgeon and Moody*, 21–51. Downers Grove: InterVarsity, 2005.
Becker, Sascha O., and Ludger Woessmann. "Was Weber Wrong? A Human Capital Theory of Protestant Economic History." *Quarterly Journal of Economics* 124 (2009) 531–96.
Becker, Sascha O., et al. "Causes and Consequences of the Protestant Reformation." Warwick Economics Research Paper Series 1105. January 2016.
Bell, Skip, ed. *Servants & Friends: A Biblical Theology of Leadership*. Berrien Springs, MI: Andrews University Press, 2014.
Berman, Harold J. *Law and Revolution*. Vol. 2, *The Impact of the Protestant Reformations on the Western Legal Tradition*. Cambridge: Harvard University Press, 2003.
———. "Religious Foundations of Law in the West: An Historical Perspective." *Journal of Law and Religion* 1 (1983) 3–43.
———. "The Spiritualization of Secular Law: The Impact of the Lutheran Reformation." *Journal of Law and Religion* 14 (2000) 313–49.
Blackaby, Henry, and Richard Blackaby. *Spiritual Leadership: Moving People on to God's Agenda*. Nashville: B&H, 2001.
Bonhoeffer, Dietrich. *Ethics*. Edited by Ilse Tödt et al. Translated by Reinhard Krauss et al. Dietrich Bonhoeffer Works 6. Minneapolis: Fortress, 2005.
———. *The Cost of Discipleship*. New York: Touchstone, 1995.
———. *Theological Education at Finkenwalde: 1935–1937*. Edited by Victoria J. Barnett and Barbara Wojhoski. Translated by Douglas W. Stott. Dietrich Bonhoeffer Works 14. Minneapolis: Fortress, 2013.
Bopart, Tim, et al. "Protestantism and Education: Reading (the Bible) and Other Skills." *Economic Inquiry* 52 (2014) 874–95.

Bibliography

Bornkamm, Heinrich. *Luther in Mid-Career, 1521–1530*. London: Darton, Longman & Todd, 1983.

Brown, Perry. "Preaching from the Print Shop." *Christian History*, issue 34, 1992.

———. "Profit-Hungry Printers." *Christian History*, issue 34, 1992.

Bruce, Steve. *Did Protestantism Create Democracy*. London: Cass, 2004.

Burns, James MacGregor. *Leadership*. New York: Harper, 1978.

Depree, Max. *Leadership Is an Art*. New York: Currency, 2004.

De Roover, Jakob, and S. N. Balagangadhara. "John Locke, Christian Liberty, and the Predicament of Liberal Toleration." *Political Theory* 36 (2008) 523–49.

DeRusha, Michelle. *Katharina & Martin: The Radical Marriage of a Runaway Nun and a Renegade Monk*. Grand Rapids: Baker, 2017.

Edwards, Mark U., Jr. "After the Revolution." *Christian History*, issue 39, 1993.

———. *Printing Propaganda, and Martin Luther*. Berkeley: University of California Press, 1994.

Ekelund, Robert, et al. "An Economic Analysis of the Protestant Reformation." *Journal of Political Economy* 110 (2002) 646–71.

Frame, John M. *A History of Western Philosophy and Theology*. 1st ed. Phillipsburg, NJ: P&R, 2015.

Galli, Mark. "Did You Know?" *Christian History*, issue 115, 2015.

———. "A Monk Marries." *Christian History*, issue 39, 1993.

George, Bill, and Peter Sims. *True North: Discover Your Authentic Leadership*. San Francisco: Jossey-Bass, 2003.

George, Timothy. "Ad Fontes!" In *Reading Scripture with the Reformers*, 44–73. Downers Grove: InterVarsity, 2011.

———. "Dr. Luther's Theology." *Christian History*, issue 34, 1992.

———. *Theology of the Reformers*. Nashville: Broadman, 1988.

Gill, Roger. *Theory and Practice of Leadership*. Thousand Oaks, CA: Sage, 2013.

Gonzalez, J. L. *Story of Christianity: The Early Church to the Present Day*. Peabody, MA: Prince, 2010.

Greenleaf, Robert. *The Servant as Leader*. Atlanta: Greenleaf Center for Servant Leadership, 2008.

Gregory, Brad S. *The Unintended Reformation: How a Religious Revolution Secularized Society*. Cambridge: Belknap of Harvard University Press, 2012.

Gritsch, Eric W. "Martin Luther and Violence: A Reappraisal of a Neuralgic Theme." *Sixteenth Century Journal* 3 (1972) 37–55.

———. *Martin Luther's Anti-Semitism: Against His Better Judgment*. Grand Rapids: Eerdmans, 2012.

———. *The Wit of Martin Luther*. Minneapolis: Fortress, 2006.

Guinness, Os. *The Call: Finding and Fulfilling the Central Purpose of Your Life*. Nashville: Word, 1998.

Haemig, Mary J., ed. "The Invocavit Sermons." In *The Annotated Luther*, 4:7–46. Minneapolis: Fortress, 2015.

Harrington, Joel F., and Helmut Walser Smith. "Confessionalization, Community, and State Building in Germany, 1555–1870." *Journal of Modern History* 69 (1997) 77–101.

Heifetz, Ronald A. *Leadership Without Easy Answers*. Cambridge: Harvard University Press, 1994.

Bibliography

Heifetz, Ronald A., and Donald L. Laurie. "The Work of Leadership." In *Harvard Business Review on Breakthrough Leadership*, edited by Daniel Goleman et al., 131–40. Boston: Harvard Business School Press, 2001.

Heifetz, Ronald A., and Marty Linsky. *Leadership on the Line*. Boston: Harvard Business School Press, 2002.

Heifetz, Ronald A., and R. Sinder. "Political Leadership: Managing the Public's Problem Solving." In *The Power of Public Ideas*, edited by Robert Reich, 179–204. London: Harvard University Press, 1989.

Heifetz, Ronald A., et al. *The Practice of Adaptive Leadership*. Boston: Harvard Business School Press, 2009.

Hendel, Kurt K. "The Smalcald Articles." In *The Annotated Luther*, vol. 2, *Word and Faith*, edited by Kirsi Stjerna, 417–78. Minneapolis: Fortress, 2015.

Hendrix, Scott A. "Legends about Luther." *Christian History*, issue 34, 1992.

———. "Luther's Impact on the Sixteenth Century." *Sixteenth Century Journal* 16 (1985) 3–14.

———. *Martin Luther: Visionary Reformer*. New Haven: Yale University Press, 2015.

Herman, Stewart W. "Luther, Law, and Social Covenants: Cooperative Self-Obligation in the Reconstruction of Lutheran Ethics." *Journal of Religious Ethics* 25 (1997) 257–75.

Hillerbrand, Hans J., ed. "Christian Life in the World." In *The Annotated Luther*, 5:281–334. Minneapolis: Fortress, 2015.

———. *The Protestant Reformation*. New York: Walker, 1968.

Hillerbrand, Hans J., et al., eds. "Word and Faith." In *The Annotated Luther*, vol. 2. Minneapolis: Fortress, 2015.

Howell, Don N., Jr. *Servants of the Servant: A Biblical Theology of Leadership*. Eugene, OR: Wipf & Stock, 2003.

Jacobs, H. E., and A. Spaeth. *Works of Martin Luther: With Introductions and Notes*. Grand Rapids: Baker, 1982.

Jacobsen, Herbert K. "Martin Luther's Early Years: Did You Know?" *Christian History*, issue 34, 1992.

Jones, Galen. "A Theological Comparison between Social Science Models and a Biblical Perspective of Servant Leadership." PhD diss., Southern Baptist Theological Seminary, 2012.

Keller, Timothy. *Every Good Endeavor*. New York: Penguin, 2013.

Kittelson, James M. "The Accidental Revolutionary." *Christian History*, issue 34, 1992.

Kittelson, James M., and Hans H. Wiersma. *Luther the Reformer*. Minneapolis: Fortress, 2016.

Kolb, Robert. *Martin Luther as Prophet, Teacher, and Hero*. Grand Rapids: Baker, 1999.

Kolb, Robert, and Charles P. Arand. *The Genius of Luther's Theology: A Wittenberg Way of Thinking for the Contemporary Church*. Grand Rapids: Baker Academic, 2008.

Kolb, Robert, and Timothy Wengert. *The Book of Concord: The Confessions of the Evangelical Lutheran Church*. Minneapolis: Fortress, 2000.

Kotter, John. *Leading Change*. Boston: Harvard Business School Press, 1996.

Kouzes, James, and Barry Posner. *Leadership Challenge*. 3rd ed. San Francisco: Jossey-Bass, 2002.

Kurtz, Johann. *Church History*. Translated by John MacPherson. Vol. 2. New York: Funk & Wagnalls, 1889.

Bibliography

Lawson, Seven. "A Mighty Fortress Is Our God: Luther as a Man of Conflict." In *The Legacy of Luther*, edited by R.C Sproul and Stephen J. Nichols, 32–52. Sanford, FL: Reformation Trust, 2016.

Lenfant, Jacques. *The History of the Council of Constance*. Vol. 1. Amsterdam, 1727.

Lewin, Kurt. *Field Theory in Social Science: Selected Theoretical Papers*. Edited by D. Cartwright. New York: Harper & Row, 1951.

Lewis, C. S. *The Great Divorce: A Dream*. New York: HarperOne, 2001.

Lindberg, Carter. *The European Reformations*. Oxford: Blackwell, 1996.

Locke, John. *A Letter Concerning Toleration*. Translated by William Popple. 1689. http://socserv2.socsci.mcmaster.ca/econ/ugcm/3ll3/locke/toleration.pdf.

Lohrmann, Martin. *Book of Harmony: Spirit and Service in the Lutheran Confessions*. Minneapolis: Fortress, 2016.

Lohse, Bernhard. *Martin Luther's Theology: Its Historical and Systematic Development*. Translated and edited by Roy A. Harrisville. Minneapolis: Fortress, 2011.

———. *Martin Luther's Basic Theological Writings*. Edited by William R. Russell and Timothy F. Lull. 3rd ed. Minneapolis: Fortress, 2012.

———. *Luther's Works*. American ed. 55 vols. Edited by Jaroslav Pelikan and Helmut T. Lehman. Philadelphia: Fortress, 1955–86.

MacArthur, John. *Slave: The Hidden Truth about Your Identity in Christ*. Nashville: Nelson, 2010.

MacKenzie, Cameron. "The Evangelical Character of Martin Luther's Faith." In *The Emergence of Evangelicalism*, edited by Michael A. G. Haykin and Kenneth J. Stewart, 171–98. Nottingham, UK: Apollos, 2008.

Maddox, Graham. "The Secular Reformation and the Influence of Machiavelli." *Journal of Religion* 82 (2002) 539–62.

Manetsch, Scott. "The Man in the Middle: Luther among the Reformers." In *The Legacy of Luther*, edited by R. C. Sproul and Stephen J. Nichols, 213–34. Sanford, FL: Reformation Trust, 2016.

Marty, M. E. *October 31, 1517: Martin Luther and the Day That Changed the World*. Brewster, MA: Paraclete, 2016.

Maxfield, John A. "Selected Letters of Pastoral and Spiritual Counsel." In *The Annotated Luther*, vol. 4, *Pastoral Writings*, edited by Mary Jane Haemig, 429–74. Minneapolis: Fortress, 2016.

McGrath, Alistair. *Christianity's Dangerous Idea: The Protestant Revolution—A History from the Sixteenth Century to the Twenty-First*. New York: HarperOne, 2007.

———. *Reformation Thought*. Oxford: Blackwell, 1999.

Methuen, Charlotte. *Luther and Calvin: Religious Revolutionaries*. Oxford: Lion Hudson, 2011.

Mitchell, Joshua. "Protestant Thought and Republican Spirit: How Luther Enchanted the World." *American Political Science Review* 86 (1992) 688–95.

Montover, Nathan. "The Political and Temporal Dimensions of Luther's Doctrine of the Priesthood of All Believers: A Case Study." PhD diss., Lutheran School of Theology at Chicago, 2008.

Mullet, Michael A. *Martin Luther*. London: Routledge, 2004.

Nestingen, James A. *Martin Luther: A Life*. Minneapolis: Augsburg Fortress, 2003.

Niebuhr, Reinhold. *The Nature and Destiny of Man*. New York: Scribner, 1953.

Niewold, Jack. "Incarnational Leadership: Towards a Distinctly Christian Theory of Leadership." PhD diss., Regent University, 2006.

Bibliography

Noll, Mark. *Turning Points: Decisive Moments in the History of Christianity*. 3rd ed. Grand Rapids: Baker Academic, 2012.

Northouse, Peter. *Leadership Theory and Practice*. Los Angeles, CA: Sage, 2010.

Oberman, Heiko A. "Fool in Rome." *Christian History*, issue 34, 1992.

Old, Hughes Oliphant. "The Age of the Reformation." In *The Reading and Preaching of the Scriptures in the Worship of the Christian Church*, 4:3–42. Grand Rapids: Eerdmans, 2002.

Ozment, Steven. "Reinventing Family Life." *Christian History*, issue 39, 1993.

Packer, J. I. *Weakness Is the Way: Life with Christ Our Strength*. Wheaton, IL: Crossway, 2013.

Peterson, Eugene H. *Five Smooth Stones for Pastoral Work*. Grand Rapids: 1996.

———. *Working the Angles: The Shape of Pastoral Integrity*. Grand Rapids: Eerdmans, 1987.

Pettegree, Andrew. *Brand Luther: 1517, Printing, and the Making of the Reformation*. New York: Penguin, 2015.

———. *How an Unheralded Monk Turned His Small Town into a Center of Publishing, Made Himself the Most Famous Man in Europe-and Started the Protestant Reformation*. New York: Penguin, 2015.

Philpott, Daniel. "The Religious Roots of Modern International Relations." *World Politics* 52 (2000) 206–45.

Plueddemann, James E. *Leading Across Cultures: Effective Ministry and Mission in the Global Church*. Downers Grove: IVP Academic, 2009.

Rankin, Alex. "Dietrich Bonhoeffer, a Modern Martyr: Taking a Stand Against the State Gone Mad." *History Teacher* 40 (2006) 111–22.

Rath, Tom. *StrengthsFinder 2.0*. New York: Gallup, 2007.

Robbert, George S. "Recommended Resources." *Christian History*, issue 34, 1992.

Rup, E. Gordon, and Philip S. Watson, eds. *Luther and Erasmus: Free Will and Salvation*. Philadelphia: Westminster, 1969.

Sanneh, Lamin. *Translating the Message*. New York: Orbis, 1989.

Sendjaya, Sen, and James C. Sarros. "Servant Leadership: Its Origin, Development, and Application in Organizations." *Journal of Leadership & Organizational Studies* 9 (2002) 57–64.

Sockness, Brent W. "Luther's Two Kingdoms Revisited: A Response to Reinhold Niebuhr's Criticism of Luther." *Journal of Religious Ethics* 20 (1992) 93–110.

Soper, J. Christopher. "Differing Perspectives on Politics among Religious Traditions." In *In God We Trust?*, edited by Corwin E. Smidt, 13–24. Grand Rapids: Baker Academic, 2001.

Sproul, R. C., and Stephen J. Nichols. eds. *The Legacy of Luther*. Sanford, FL: Reformation Trust, 2016.

Stroup, John. "Political Theology and Secularization Theory in Germany, 1918–1939: Emanuel Hirsch as a Phenomenon of His Time." *Harvard Theological Review* 80 (1987) 321–68.

Thigpen, Paul. "A Gallery—Family Album." *Christian History*, issue 39, 1993.

———. "A Gallery of Friends and Enemies." *Christian History*, issue 34, 1992.

Trueman, Carl R. "Life and Death in This Earthly Realm: Government, Calling, and Family." In *Luther on the Christian Life*, 175–94. Wheaton, IL: Crossway, 2015.

Weber, Max. *The Protestant Ethic and the Spirit of Capitalism*. Translated by Stephen Kalberg. London: Routledge, 2013.

Bibliography

Wengert, Timothy J. "The Freedom of a Christian." In *The Annotated Luther*, vol. 1, *The Roots of Reform*, edited by Timothy J. Wengert, 467–538. Minneapolis: Fortress, 2015.

———. "The Small Catechism." In *The Annotated Luther*, vol. 4, *Pastoral Writings*, edited by Mary Jane Haemig, 201–52. Minneapolis: Fortress, 2016.

Whelchel, Hugh. *How Then Should We Work?* Bloomington, IN: WestBow, 2012.

Whitford, David M. "Cura Religionis or Two Kingdoms: The Late Luther on Religion and the State in Lectures on Genesis." *Church History* 73 (2004) 41–62.

Wilkes, Gene C. *Jesus on Leadership: Timeless Wisdom on Servant Leadership*. Carol Stream, IL: Tyndale, 1998.

Willard, Dallas. *Renovation of the Heart: Putting on the Character of Christ*. Colorado Springs: NavPress, 2002.

Wilson, H. S. "Luther on Preaching as God Speaking." In *The Pastoral Luther: Essays on Martin Luther's Practical Theology*, edited by Timothy J. Wengert, 100–114. Grand Rapids: Eerdmans, 2009.

Wingren, Gustav. *Luther on Vocation*. Translated by Carl C. Rasmussen. Philadelphia: Muhlenberg, 1957.

Witte, John. *Law and Protestantism: The Legal Teachings of the Lutheran Reformation*. Cambridge: Cambridge University Press, 2002.

———. "Law, Religion, and Human Rights: A Historical Protestant Perspective." *Journal of Religious Ethics* 26 (1998) 257–62.

———. *Religion and the American Constitutional Experiment*. Boulder, CO: Westview, 2011.

Wolin, Sheldon S. "Politics and Religion: Luther's Simplistic Imperative." *American Political Science Review* 50 (1956) 24–42.

Wood, James E. "Christianity and the State." *Journal of the American Academy of Religion* 35 (1967) 257–70.

Yukl, Gary. *Leadership in Organizations*. Upper Saddle River, NJ: Pearson Prentice Hall, 2006.

Zecher, Henry. "The Bible Translation That Rocked the World." *Christian History*, issue 34, 1992.